W9-ARB-181

Spike Lee

Contemporary Film Directors

Edited by Justus Nieland and Jennifer Fay

The Contemporary Film Directors series provides concise, well-written introductions to directors from around the world and from every level of the film industry. Its chief aims are to broaden our awareness of important artists, to give serious critical attention to their work, and to illustrate the variety and vitality of contemporary cinema. Contributors to the series include an array of internationally respected critics and academics. Each volume contains an incisive critical commentary, an informative interview with the director, and a detailed filmography.

A list of books in the series appears
at the end of this book.

Spike Lee |

Todd McGowan

UNIVERSITY
OF
ILLINOIS
PRESS
URBANA,
CHICAGO,
AND
SPRINGFIELD

Frontispiece: Spike Lee as Mars Blackmon
in *She's Gotta Have It*.

Library of Congress Cataloging-in-Publication Data
McGowan, Todd.
Spike Lee / by Todd McGowan.
p.   cm. — (Contemporary film directors)
Includes bibliographical references and index.
Includes filmography.
ISBN 978-0-252-03814-3 (hardcover : alk. paper) —
ISBN 978-0-252-07961-0 (pbk. : alk. paper) —
ISBN 978-0-252-09540-5 (e-book)
1. Lee, Spike—Criticism and interpretation.
I. Title.
PN1998.3.L44M35   2014
791.4302'33092—dc23   2013023553

For Jonathan Mulrooney,
a true friend of excess

Contents |

Acknowledgments

Thanks to Justus Nieland and Jennifer Fay for asking me to write this book. Without their prompting, I would never have undertaken it. They also provided a thorough reading of the manuscript that permitted me to clarify many ambiguities. I owe a debt of gratitude to Daniel Nasset at the University of Illinois Press, who stood by a theoretical work even when this encountered some resistance. Many thanks also to Susan White for her generous reading of the book and her many suggestions. This book would not have been possible without the generous permission of Hollywood.com to publish an interview with Spike Lee that appears on their Web site. Thanks also to Lisa Collins, the interviewer, who was very patient throughout the process and worked diligently on editing the interview.

Thanks to Jonathan Mulrooney, Sheila Kunkle, Fabio Vighi, Hugh Manon, Frances Restuccia, Jennifer Friedlander, Henry Krips, and Slavoj Žižek. They have each shaped my thinking on psychoanalysis and cinema.

As always, Walter Davis, Paul Eisenstein, and Hilary Neroni provided the background without which nothing would have been possible for me.

Spike Lee |

Confronted with Too Much |

Spike Lee is a filmmaker of excess. Excess characterizes each of his films—through unconventional shots, extreme characters, improbable scenes, and many other ways. Lee's films employ these types of excess to intervene in critical issues that trouble the contemporary world—the question of the subject's singularity, the role that fantasy plays in structuring our reality, the political impact of passion, the power of paranoia in shaping social relations, the damage that the insistence on community inflicts, the problem of transcendence, and the struggles of the spectator. Above all, Lee is known for being a political filmmaker, and I contend that the concept of excess holds the key to understanding the politics of his films. The different sections of the book will explore how excess has enabled Lee to create a varied corpus of films that treat a broad spectrum of fundamental social and political problems.

Within the study of film, excess has a precise definition. It is what goes beyond the narrative requirements of a film and thereby draws the spectator's attention to form. But excess is also operative throughout the social order, as many thinkers have recognized. It disrupts the smooth functioning of society and makes evident the failure of all elements to fit together. The social order suffers from the disturbance of excess because it never forms a consistent and coherent whole. In this sense, excess is Sigmund Freud's unconscious, Karl Marx's class struggle, Simone de Beauvoir's sexual difference, Frantz Fanon's violence, and many related theoretical formulations of the incompleteness of society. The exploration of excess in Spike Lee's films shows his position among these thinkers and reveals the breadth of his filmic contribution not only to the history of cinema but also to the most pressing questions of our time.

Lee's films show that, as subjects, we are defined by what exceeds our social identity, and they also make evident that what exceeds our typical frame of reference is identical to the passion that animates us. This is the fundamental contention of psychoanalysis and what separates it from recent theorizing about the problem of affect within communal life. Psychoanalytic thought defines the subject as a singular excess irreducible to any individual identity or social group. Our passion or mode of enjoyment is excessive in relation to the social structure and even to our sense of who we are. In short, every passion is an excessive passion. It is not simply an affect that we have—one among many—but rather what constitutes us as subjects.

A subject doesn't simply occupy an individual or group identity but relates to this identity through a passionate response (most often either embrace or rejection, but sometimes indifference). Passion exists in the distance that separates subjects from the identities that they inhabit. The social order can use this passion to mobilize subjects, and in this process, passion becomes a source of homogeneity rather than singularity. When passion functions as a source of social identification, it homogenizes subjects by focusing each subject on the same object. But this mobilization of passion is always a fraught enterprise. Passion necessarily exceeds the limits that the social order would place on it, which often leads it to disrupt the social order employing it. Passion doesn't fit within the narratives that we use to understand ourselves and our actions, and yet it is, in the last instance, determinative.

We act, as Lee reveals, on the basis of this passion. This is why Nola Darling (Tracy Camilla Johns), the heroine of Lee's first feature, *She's Gotta Have It* (1986), cannot abandon her passion to have multiple sexual partners despite her recognition of the difficulties that this excess creates. Nola Darling's passion separates her from the possibility of a monogamous relationship, just as passion in other Lee films estranges characters from their community. When critics like Douglas Kellner or Sharon Willis note Lee's inability to depict successful communities, they miss the political possibilities of his anticommunitarian focus on excess. By isolating our various forms of disturbing passion, Lee forces spectators to confront their unconscious investment in what they consciously declaim—violence, paranoia, racism, sexism, oppression, and so on. As a result, the films move spectators from their usual viewing positions. It is impossible to watch a Spike Lee film in the way that one watches a typical Hollywood film. A Lee film forces spectators not only to see differently but to confront their own unconscious, whether this unconscious is associated with their own singularity as subjects, their racism, their membership in a community, or whatever else.

The aim of Lee's films is not to shame viewers into an abandonment of their passion. His is not a moral cinema in the traditional sense, even though he often presents characters acting in the worst ways that would seem to invite moral judgment. Instead, the films encourage the spectator to identify with this passion in order to create a new way of relating to it. Passion, as Lee's films illustrate it, is not equivalent to pleasure and does not bring happiness. Instead, it is a burden, a surplus of pleasure that we suffer and that derails our pursuit of happiness. As Alenka Zupančič describes it in her *Ethics of the Real*, "[I]t is not simply the mode of enjoyment of the neighbour, of the other, that is strange to me. The heart of the problem is that I experience my own enjoyment (which emerges along with the enjoyment of the other, and is even indissociable from it) as strange and hostile" (225). It is clear how another's enjoyment or passion might function as a burden or source of unhappiness, but this same quality haunts my own passion as well.

At the same time, passion makes one's life worth living. Passion is excessive and thus burdensome—it consistently produces personal and social self-destruction—but it also animates our existence. As the French psychoanalyst Jacques Lacan insists, our passion or mode of enjoyment— what he calls "jouissance"—precipitates any investment in the world. In his essay "The Subversion of the Subject," Lacan states, "It is Jouissance whose absence would render the universe vain" (694). When people feel as if their lives have no meaning, what they miss is not the significance of their actions but the passion to act. Passion is not a value added to life but the basis of what makes life worth living. Passion or enjoyment is the sine qua non of the subject's existence, but it typically leads to exclusions from the social order. Fascism, for instance, mobilizes passion for the sake of violent exclusions. In this vein, Lee's films often depict the nefarious effects of passion as it manifests itself in racism or paranoia. In order to attach themselves to an identity and seek out a sense of belonging, subjects display their passion for the identity and the exclusions that define it. We see how passion fuels an outburst of racist speech or even, more remarkably, the institutional failure to respond to the disaster of Hurricane Katrina. The power of Lee's documentaries on the failure to act after Hurricane Katrina stems directly from their depiction of the passion involved with the neglect of those affected by the catastrophe. A passionate indifference to the citizens of New Orleans manifests itself throughout *When the Levees Broke* (2006) and *If God Is Willing and da Creek Don't Rise* (2010). The social structures of racism emerge and thrive through the passion of the subjects who sustain them.

That said, implicit in Lee's films is the idea that a different mode of relating to excess is possible. Rather than exploding in violent outbursts of racism as in *Do the Right Thing* (1989) or *Jungle Fever* (1991), excess can take on another political valence and become the source for emancipation. Lee's depiction of excess is always a complex portrayal of how it works in contemporary society. Excess is formal in its essence and has no inherent political bent. It can lead us toward acts of exclusion, or it can enable us to revolt against an oppressive situation. It can fuel the actions of the Ku Klux Klan and those of the civil rights movement. Lee shows excess in all its forms, but even in the negative portrayals, his films make clear that excess is what gives our existence what value it has. Without excess, life becomes empty and unlivable. Consequently, the struggle with excess colors our entire being, and we must find a way of relating to it that doesn't involve us in racist violence or other types of brutal oppression.

In the 1970s and early 1980s, film theorists began to think about the role of excess in the cinema. The most notable of these theorists were Roland Barthes, Stephen Heath, and Kristin Thompson. Though their positions on excess were not identical and their terminology was distinct, they did adopt a similar approach. For each of them, filmic excess opposes itself to narrative and to signification; it is what doesn't have a clear function in the filmic narrative or a clear meaning for the film's signification.

Thompson establishes a straightforward opposition between what serves a narrative function in a film and what doesn't. As she sees it, excess exceeds narrative motivation and critical understanding. It challenges the meaningful wholeness that filmic narrative aims to produce. Thompson claims, "Excess is not only counternarrative, but it is also counterunity. To discuss it may be to invite the partial disintegration of a coherent reading" (293). Excess doesn't fit within the structure of meaning, and as a result, it resists all analysis. All that the critic can do is point it out and demonstrate how it challenges possible avenues of interpretation. Thompson's view that excess opposes meaning follows from Roland Barthes's theory of narrative.

Barthes was the first to draw attention to excess, and he did so in the context of the semiotic analysis of cinema. In this analysis (which focuses on Sergei Eisenstein), he identifies three levels of meaning—an informational meaning, a symbolic meaning, and an obtuse or third meaning. This obtuse meaning doesn't fall within the domain of semiotic analysis but exists exterior to it. Barthes notes that "the obtuse meaning is outside (articulated) language while nevertheless within interlocution" (61). The critic can identify the excess of the obtuse meaning but cannot reduce it to any definite signified content. It doesn't provide information for the spectator, nor does it have a symbolic resonance.

Barthes locates the obtuse meaning within the act of filmic production, and this becomes pivotal for Stephen Heath's analysis. Heath's description of the filmic system makes clear that its aim is containing rather than highlighting the excess of the act of production over what has been produced. He claims, "The system achieves a reflection, images of unity, but, as production, is in excess of those images" (117). In spite of the visibility of productive excess, Heath argues, "the narrative offers to contain its production" (117). This prioritizing of the produced over the act of production leads cinema to function as an ideological mechanism. The problem with cinematic excess is that it doesn't stand a chance against narrative's absolute hegemony. Just as the commodity hides the labor that produces it, and the capitalist's profit hides the worker's creation of surplus value, the film renders its production invisible to the spectator.

During this heyday for the theorization of cinematic excess, no theorist made the connection—a connection evident throughout Spike Lee's films—between excess and passion. The theorists maintain excess on the level of production and work rather than identifying it with passion. This same association becomes apparent in Peter Wollen's discussion of the contrast between avant-garde and Hollywood cinema. The excess of Jean-Luc Godard's avant-garde cinema, according to Wollen, attempts to dissatisfy the spectator by privileging production at the expense of narrative entertainment. For the early theorists of excess, excess is not the site where we experience our passion but the site of the production of surplus value.

The problem with this identification of excess and production is that it fails to account for the pull that excess has on us. When he initially theorizes excess, Barthes comes closest to this recognition, as he notes that the obtuse meaning draws him to a film beyond the information and symbolism that the film imparts. But this doesn't go far enough. To understand Spike Lee's films and the role that excess plays in them, a new theory—one that focuses on the intimate link between excess and passion—is required. This would be a theory of excess rooted not in narrative theory or Marxism (like the earlier theories) but in the fundamental tenets of psychoanalysis. Psychoanalysis takes the disruptiveness of passion or enjoyment as its point of departure. Sigmund Freud discovers psychoanalysis when he encounters subjects who should be satisfied but are not, and he finally comes to see a fundamental link between satisfaction and suffering, a link that results from the excessive nature of the subject's satisfaction. Subjects don't only satisfy themselves but instead suffer their satisfaction. The subject never fits properly in the place assigned for it in the signifying structure. This failure to fit leaves the subject unable simply to experience pleasure without falling into excess.

Rather than identifying excess with the act of production, I contend that we must instead identify it with enjoyment that teems around the edge of the structure of signification. What exceeds use within a signifying act provides the source of our investment in signification. For psychoanalysis, passion or enjoyment exceeds the narratives of community and identity that the social order produces. Even if these narratives try to mobilize passions, passions necessarily escape their control and interrupt their smooth functioning. Passion—even the passion for a normal life—involves an overinvestment that transcends the limits of the social structure. Passion is a form of relation to identity that necessarily exceeds all identity.

In terms of cinema, when we encounter excess, the content overflows into the form and disturbs the illusory security of spectatorship. Formal excess, especially as Lee employs it, attempts to touch the spectator's own relationship to the images on the screen and to expose the passion inhering in this relationship. One enjoys a Lee film because it goes too far, and then one either embraces or retreats from this enjoyment. Excess in the cinema is inseparable from the question of how we enjoy and the relationship we take up to our enjoyment.

Enjoyment exceeds narrative because of the subject's lack of identity with the world of sense. The subject is not the product of a successful ideological interpellation but the irreducible mode of enjoying that the ideological narrative of sense can never fully incorporate. We enjoy what doesn't fit, the stumbling blocks of sense, rather than sense itself. This is why mysteries or blockages of sense—detective novels, word puzzles, the opacity of another's desire, and so on—have an inherent appeal for us. We seek out the disruption of sense and meaning rather than its smooth flow. What we encounter in excess, as its early theorists rightly point out, has no signifying function, but it does have the effect of rendering the world of signification enjoyable, which is what these theorists miss and Lee's films make evident.

Passion or enjoyment in this sense derives from what Freud calls the death drive: we seek out obstacles and we undermine ourselves because this enables us to enjoy in a way that is impossible when our existence seems stable. The psychoanalytic theorist Joan Copjec describes this excess that drives the subject onward as the object of its drive, the engine for all of the subject's activity. She notes, "Some inherent obstacle—the *object* of the drive—simultaneously *brakes* the drive and *breaks it up,* curbs it, thus preventing it from reaching its aim" (34). The excess that disrupts the flow of significance in our social reality drives us as subjects. Without this obstacle or kernel of nonsense, we would become static beings stuck in an unending cycle of need and fulfillment. Even though excess remains irreducible to signification, it nonetheless provides the lifeblood for this structure. Subjects continue to play out their social roles and to immerse themselves within signification because the passion that exceeds the signifier drives them onward. This is precisely what Spike Lee grasps in his films, and it differentiates him not only from Hollywood filmmaking but also from the major anti-Hollywood filmic movements throughout the world.

Though counter-cinema and the various new waves in filmmaking often oppose themselves to the coherent narrative structure of classical Hollywood filmmaking by turning to excess, they do not do so to expose passion in the way that Lee does. Instead, in keeping with the early theorists of cinematic excess, they tend to use formal excess to highlight the act of production. This occurs in Jean-Luc Godard's *Week-end* (1967), where the lengthy tracking shot of the traffic jam and the obtrusive use of intertitles make it clear that we are watching a film, and at the conclusion of Abbas Kiarostami's *A Taste of Cherry* (1997), as Kiarostami includes the crew's sound check within the film itself. These moments of formal excess force the spectator to contend with the film as a production rather than wrestle with the events depicted within the diegetic world.

Other anti-Hollywood filmmakers identify Hollywood with excessive spectacle and thus attempt to strip excess from their films in response. This approach first appears most prominently in the early films of Italian neorealism, but it perhaps reaches its unsurpassable zenith with Chantal Akerman's *Jeanne Dielman, 23 Quai du Commerce, 1080 Bruxelles* (1975). Akerman creates a film that captures the monotony of the housewife's life. Even the occasional forays into prostitution remain firmly ensconced within a thoroughly homogeneous and rigid formal structure that bespeaks the absence of any passion within the typical housewife's existence. Following the tradition of Italian neorealism and other national cinemas, Akerman combats Hollywood's promulgation of excessive spectacle by creating a minimalist cinema. Her political intervention involves an assault on excess. In direct contrast to both this strategy and the deployment of excess by counter-cinema, Spike Lee turns excess in a different direction by associating it with the disruptiveness of enjoyment.

Lee began as a filmmaker at a nadir of African American filmmaking. After the end of the blaxploitation era in the 1970s, there were almost no opportunities for African American filmmakers. As Lee points out in *That's My Story and I'm Sticking to It,* his autobiography cowritten with Kaleem Aftab, "People didn't believe me when I told them that I was going to be a filmmaker. . . . They probably couldn't name any African-American filmmakers then. The only one working at the time was Michael Schultz" (12). Schultz was not a prominent figure in American cinema, though he did direct *Car Wash* (1976), *Greased Lightning* (1977), and *Sgt. Pepper's Lonely Hearts Club Band* (1978), a tribute to the Beatles. There were other black filmmakers working in the margins without Hollywood funding, but their films did not garner much of an audience, which led them to produce only a few films. This was the case with Melvin Van Peebles and Charles Burnett. But even in this era, Lee was able to gain a foothold in a white-dominated industry and make films that, from the beginning, would establish him as one of the great visionaries in the medium.

After growing up as the oldest of five children in a family in Brooklyn, Lee went to Morehouse College in Atlanta, where he took an interest in filmmaking and began to make his own amateur films. While at Morehouse, he made a short entitled *Last Hustle in Brooklyn* (1977), which displays the fascination for New York City life that would become central in his feature films. From there, Lee went to film school at New York University, where he made *The Answer* (1980), a film about a black filmmaker being commissioned to remake D. W. Griffith's racist classic *Birth of a Nation* (1915), and *Sarah* (1981), a film depicting a family Thanksgiving dinner that Lee claims to have made for his grandmother.

Lee's foundational film at New York University was his final student project, a sixty-minute film that cost ten thousand dollars to make called *Joe's Bed-Stuy Barbershop: We Cut Heads* (1983). The film won the Student Academy Award and caught the attention of Nelson George, the managing editor of *Billboard* magazine, who helped to promote it. This made possible Lee's first feature, which was to be *The Messenger,* but a lack of funding for this project caused it to fall through. This led to Lee's breakthrough debut, *She's Gotta Have It,* which focuses on a sexually voracious woman who cannot settle for a monogamous relationship, despite the efforts of her three lovers. Shot over a twelve-day period on a starting budget of twenty thousand dollars, the film became a success from its San Francisco premiere onward. The total budget for the film was $175,000, but it made $7.1 million at the box office. Its popular and critical success established Spike Lee as an original figure in the world of American cinema, and it marked the first feature film of his production company, 40 Acres and a Mule, named for the quickly abandoned policy established by General Sherman at the close of the Civil War that offered land and a mule to emancipated slaves. This production company would become synonymous with Lee and produce all of his subsequent films.

For his first feature, Lee used unknown actors, including Tracy Camilla Johns in the lead role, because he couldn't afford established performers. Budgetary constraints also led Lee to cast himself in one of the starring roles in the film and to edit the film. He collaborated again with the cinematographer from *Joe's Bed-Stuy Barbershop: We Cut Heads*, Ernest Dickerson, who would go on to shoot all of Lee's early films and then become himself a director, as well as Barry Brown, who helped Lee with the sound on this film and then went on to be Lee's principal editor. Lee's father, Bill Lee, provided the music, as he also would for *School Daze* (1988), *Do the Right Thing*, and *Mo' Better Blues* (1990).

After *She's Gotta Have It*, Lee became widely known to mainstream audiences not as an up-and-coming director but as the costar with Michael Jordan in advertisements for Nike. In these commercials, Lee directs and plays Mars Blackmon, the role that he first performed in *She's Gotta Have It*. The commercials emphasize Jordan's transcendent basketball ability, and the diminutive Blackmon plays the foil for Jordan. The success of the advertisements derives from their portrayal of Jordan as a figure of excessive singularity, and in this way, there is a continuity between Lee's films and the commercials that made him famous.

Based on the success of his first film, Columbia financed *School Daze*, his follow-up feature. The film focuses on a historically black college, and Lee wanted to shoot it at Morehouse, his alma mater. But disturbed by the politics of the film and its discussion of a black college's refusal to combat apartheid by divesting from South Africa, the school denied Lee the right to shoot on campus. This is one early instance of the disruptiveness created by Lee's concern for what exceeds the limits of social and political structures. Rather than simply making a film that celebrates the black college experience, his film reveals a political controversy that disturbs the leadership at Morehouse. *School Daze* began

Lee's collaboration with his fellow Morehouse student Monty Ross, who worked as a producer on the film and continued to work with Lee until *Clockers* in 1995. With a budget of $6.5 million, the box office for the film was $14.5 million, making it a success for Columbia, despite many negative reviews and a general sense among critics that this was a step backwards from *She's Gotta Have It*.

While Lee's first two films tackled serious issues like sexuality and race, their overall tone was light. *She's Gotta Have It* is a romance with comic elements, and *School Daze* is a musical comedy. *Do the Right Thing* marks a radical turn in style. Though there are humorous moments and characters, the film deals with the deadly ramifications of racism in New York City and America. For the first time in Lee's career, excess leads to violent death, not only to failed romances. The film emerges in response to a series of incidents of racist violence that occurred in New York during the late 1980s, including the murder of Michael Griffith, a black man, by a group of Italian Americans in Howard Beach. Like most of Lee's films, *Do the Right Thing* takes place in a confined area—a small neighborhood in the Bedford-Stuyvesant section of Brooklyn. His films often confine themselves to a restricted setting to emphasize how the characters transcend place without actually leaving it.

The success of *Do the Right Thing* propelled Lee into the international spotlight. Like *School Daze*, the film had a $6.5 million budget (from Universal), but it was an incredible popular success, grossing over $37 million. *Do the Right Thing* competed for the Palme d'Or at the Cannes Film Festival, but it lost to Steven Soderbergh's debut feature, *Sex, Lies, and Videotape* (1989). Though largely overlooked by the Academy Awards, Lee did receive an Oscar nomination for Best Original Screenplay, and his film stands at number ninety-six on the American Film Institute's list of the one hundred top movies of all time. For many scholars and critics, it remains Lee's most enduring achievement.

The film was also a cultural phenomenon. Numerous television programs and newspapers devoted their attention to the film and the questions about racial injustice that it raises. But the response also often resulted in the pigeonholing of Lee himself. As Ed Guerrero points out in his excellent book-length account of the film, "With the film's release the white press broadly portrayed Spike Lee as an angry black urban youth. And by stereotyping him thus, the mainstream media were able to distort and overlook *Do the Right Thing*'s complex mediation of racial power relations, while simplistically reducing the film's complex argument to a sensational exploitation of violence" (21–22). The Nike commercials made Lee into a public figure, but *Do the Right Thing* transformed him into a controversial personality, one wrongly identified with racial hostility instead of with a thoroughgoing critique of racism, which is what the film formulates.

Lee's third feature not only gave him a visible position within popular culture; it also began several collaborations that would prove fruitful for him. It was the first Lee film to feature John Turturro, who would go on to become a mainstay in the director's films, and it marked the producer Jon Kilik's first shoot with Lee. Kilik would work consistently with Lee throughout his career, producing films such as *Clockers*, *Summer of Sam* (1999), *25th Hour* (2002), and several others. With *Do the Right Thing*, Lee entered the cinematic main stage and began his career as a filmmaker in earnest.

This film would also establish Lee's fundamental aesthetic concerns and lay down the path for his subsequent ventures. The role that excess plays in his films is fully evident in his third feature. The first films show the power that excess has in sexual desire and in intraracial hostility, but

The complex critique of racism
in *Do the Right Thing*.

its political importance becomes clear in *Do the Right Thing*. From this film onward, the role of excess in social interactions becomes paramount. Lee shows that what underlies all social encounters is an enjoyment that causes individuals to act against their own self-interest and against the interests of the society as a whole. Subjects are excessive, Lee shows, because they are driven to go beyond the confines of self and the community's good. We are subjects of an unpredictable drive rather than rationally calculating agents out to advance our well-being or to flourish.

The controversy that began with *Do the Right Thing* abated to some extent with his next film, *Mo' Better Blues*. With this film, Lee returns to the musical and constructs his own tribute to jazz. He made the film in opposition to Hollywood's prevailing image of the jazz musician, one disseminated by films like Clint Eastwood's *Bird* (1988). Rather than depicting the imploding jazz musician destroyed by drug use, *Mo' Better Blues* focuses on the musician's passion for the music and the effect of this passion on the musician and those close to him. The hero of *Mo' Better Blues* ends up in a loving family relationship rather than a drug-induced death.

The film featured the up-and-coming star Denzel Washington as the jazz musician Bleek Gilliam. This was Washington's first appearance in a Lee film, and he would go on to star in *Malcolm X* (1992), *He Got Game* (1998), and *Inside Man* (2006). Though the film did not generate the controversy of *Do the Right Thing*, it did not escape entirely unscathed. The negative depiction of two Jewish managers generated controversy and led Abraham Foxman of the Anti-Defamation League to complain about the use of anti-Semitic stereotypes. In response, Lee made public statements against anti-Semitism, but he also defended his right to portray negative Jewish characters. In his films, no character entirely escapes an excessive portrayal—or a portrayal of excess—that necessarily verges on stereotype.

One of the recurring critiques of Lee's filmmaking is his use of stereotypes, whether of black women, Italian working-class men, or Jewish business owners, as is the case in *Mo' Better Blues*. There are points at which Lee slips into blatant stereotyping, but his films run this risk because they themselves operate in the same manner as stereotypes do—by focusing on excess. The difference is that stereotypes simply display and use excess, while Lee explores its use in his films. He tries to show why the stereotype has the power that it does, though in doing so, he sometimes falls victim to the very structure that he exposes. If *Mo' Better Blues* mitigated the controversy surrounding Spike Lee, *Jungle Fever* brought it back to its earlier level. The film depicts an interracial relationship between a black man and a white woman that ultimately founders on their racial difference. The common critical indictment of the film focuses on its apparent attitude toward interracial romance. Ronald Sundstrom offers an exemplary formulation of this assessment: "[O]n the topic of interracial intimacy, Lee's movie is oddly puritanical. On this point, *Jungle Fever* is more timorous than *Guess Who's Coming to Dinner*" (159–60). But in some sense, the attention to interracial romance misses the film's overriding concern. The film chronicles various excessive attachments: the attachment to racial homogeneity, to crack, and to religion. In each case, the excess proves destructive for the characters in the film.

Lee's next film was his most extreme in terms of its length: *Malcolm X* is a three-hour-and-twenty-minute epic. The idea of making a biopic about Malcolm X had long been Lee's dream, though its fulfillment was fraught with difficulties. When Warner Brothers balked at fully financing the film, Lee had to call on prominent African Americans for financial assistance, and the final product received a mixed response. For some, it indulged the Nation of Islam too much, and for others, it unjustly depicted the Nation of Islam as the villain. Other critics attacked the film's sexism and heteronormativity. Maurice Stevens, for instance, claims that "*Malcolm X* is a film dominated by all-male spaces and predominantly male relations" (328). But the primary critique centered on the depiction of Malcolm X himself, which occasioned objections from prominent black intellectuals such as Amiri Baraka, who claimed that Lee reduces the complexities of Malcolm X to caricature. This is always the danger for a filmmaker committed to revealing excess.

Nonetheless, for many, *Malcolm X* became the crowning Spike Lee film. It also marked the end of his collaboration with the cinematographer Ernest Dickerson and brought a change in his choice of projects. Lee's subsequent films in the mid-1990s were quieter affairs, no longer grabbing the attention that his first five films did. The films that followed *Malcolm X* had multiple virtues, but they did not bring Lee back into the limelight. *Crooklyn* (1994) is a family melodrama loosely based on

Lee's own childhood, while *Clockers* allowed Lee to take on directly the drug culture of the inner city that he explores tangentially in *Jungle Fever*. Neither film had the box-office impact of Lee's earlier works, and the lack of popular success would continue with his subsequent films in the mid-1990s. Lee's two films from 1996, *Girl 6* and *Get on the Bus*, though dramatically different in tone and subject matter, both met the same box-office and critical fate. The muted reception of the depiction of the phone-sex world in *Girl 6* and a trip to the 1995 Million Man March in *Get on the Bus* made the mid-1990s a low point of Lee's filmmaking career. Though *Get on the Bus* received good reviews that *Girl 6* did not, the former shared the latter's lack of success at the box office, leading Lee to complain about the lack of black support for serious black films. In retrospect and in light of what Lee has done afterwards, however, these films gain in significance.

Lee's documentary *4 Little Girls* (1997), about the murder of four black girls in the bombing of a black church during the civil-rights movement, marked a step in a new direction that he would develop more fully in the 2000s. After the popular success of *He Got Game*, Lee's panegyric to basketball, his favorite sport, he reached a high point in his career that surpassed the early success of *Do the Right Thing*. Just as it seemed that Lee had retreated from groundbreaking films, he made in 1999 and 2000 what are perhaps his two greatest works. *Summer of Sam* and *Bamboozled* (2000) represent Lee at the height of his powers.

Both films returned Lee to controversy as well as cinematic success. Critics attacked *Summer of Sam* for its negative portrayal of Italian Americans, and *Bamboozled* depicts black characters in blackface, a technique that seemed to go too far in the minds of many critics. Even Roger Ebert, otherwise a fan of Lee's work, characterized *Bamboozled* as a failure for overshooting the mark. Despite the poor reception by audiences and critics at the time, the intervening years have been very kind to the film, and many now view it as one of Lee's masterpieces. For instance, in "*Bamboozled*: Philosophy through Blackface," Dan Flory associates Lee's film with the effect that Socrates had on Athens. He claims that like Socrates, "Lee's aim is to get us to see how we must change—think, act, and perceive our world and our place in it differently—if we are to fully live up to our professed ideals of justice and equality" (179). The power of *Bamboozled* stems from its unrelenting indictment of our capacity to be duped by racist tropes, especially at the moments when we think we have transcended them. But the film is also a critique directed at black actors and artists complicit with the perpetuation of racist stereotypes. In an interview with Allison Samuels, Lee contrasts the situation of contemporary black artists with those of the past: "My people have to wake up and realize what's going on and our responsibility in it. I mean, back in the day we didn't have a choice. Hattie McDaniel and Bojangles didn't have a choice. Nowadays we don't have to do this stuff. So anything you do is on you" (Samuels 188). Lee goes on to criticize Ving Rhames for giving his Golden Globe Award to Jack Lemmon and to attack Cuba Gooding Jr. for his minstrel-like performance—professing his love for everyone and dancing around the stage—after winning an Oscar. Gooding's celebration was for Lee an instance of the racist deployment of excessive passion.

In the 2000s, Lee made several documentaries, ranging from the comedic in *The Original Kings of Comedy* (2000), to the biographical in *Jim Brown: All American* (2002) and *Kobe Doin' Work* (2009), to the tragic in *When the Levees Broke: A Requiem in Four Acts* and *If God Is Willing and da Creek Don't Rise*. These films—especially the latter two, which chronicle the criminal neglect of New Orleans after Hurricane Katrina struck—helped to reestablish Lee as a fervent voice on the political landscape. Here, his political efforts were relatively straightforward, though he brought his concern for excess to the documentary form.

During this time, Lee also made several forays into television and directed pilots for television series, such as *Sucker Free City* (2004), though none of them were picked up by the networks. The fictional features that Lee made after *Bamboozled* reflect his full development as a filmmaker. *25th Hour* details the last hours of freedom of a convicted felon, while *Inside Man* and *Miracle at St. Anna* (2009) show Lee moving into genre filmmaking while retaining his formal inventiveness. The former is a heist film that complicates the conventions of the genre, while the latter is a war film that reveals a moment of transcendence within the confined landscape of the battlefield. In 2004, Lee directed what was probably his most dramatic failure, *She Hate Me,* an account of a man who works as a sperm donor for lesbian couples. Critics assailed the film, and audiences stayed away. But the subsequent success of *Inside Man* established Lee as an auteur capable of breathing life into a genre film, just as Christopher

Nolan recently did with the superhero film. This undoubtedly led Hollywood (specifically, Mandate Pictures) to target Lee for the American version of the South Korean success *Old Boy* (Park Chan-wook, 2003). In 2012, he returned to small-budget independent filmmaking with *Red Hook Summer*, a film made in just eighteen days.

Throughout Lee's filmmaking career, he has always been larger than his films. If his films have exemplified excess, he has as well. Most film directors do not have a public persona. Even the most famous Hollywood and foreign directors, like James Cameron and Wong Kar-wai, inhabit a relative obscurity. Lee's fame is exceptional, but it does not derive entirely from his filmmaking. The public knows him also as a fan of the New York Knicks basketball team and as an engaged political figure. As Lee himself laments, this leads to critics not taking his films seriously on their own terms. In *That's My Story and I'm Sticking to It*, Lee proclaims, "Their review of my films is 'Why I Don't Like Spike Lee.' They don't review the film. After Woody Allen went through all that shit when he married his stepdaughter I decided to read every review of his next film, and there was no mention of that. Not one. Then I read my reviews. 'Why is he jumping up and down at the Knicks games?' Why aren't they able to make the distinction between the director and the film?" (252). Discussing Lee's activity at a Knicks game during a review of a film is clearly an attempt to avoid the film itself, to focus on Lee's personal excesses in order to escape the indictment registered by the excesses of the film.

Through excess, the subject discovers its singularity and transcends its environment. Excess, as Lee depicts it, provides the possibility for a passion that one cannot find elsewhere, and it is simultaneously a site for emancipation. His films reveal the excessive attachments of various characters. The point of Lee's filmmaking is to avow such attachments so that they don't become the source of a violent or aggressive outburst, which is what occurs when one experiences oneself as excluded from the enjoyment that others seem to monopolize.

Singular Subjects

Though all of Lee's films focus on excessive attachments, they are not all explicitly political in the manner of *Do The Right Thing* or *Bamboozled*, where the focus is on racism and its social effects. In Lee's less overtly political films, he often focuses on the passion of an individual character, and this passion produces a singularity that does not fit within the prevailing cultural logic or societal definitions of identity. In any discussion of singularity, it is important to begin by distinguishing it from the liberal individuality idealized by capitalist society. In contrast to individuality, singularity marks the subject's dislocation, its estrangement from the social order. Whereas the individual has a number of qualities that define it, singularity emerges when personality disappears and a passion emerges. In this sense, singularity is not only different from individuality but its opposite. The individual sees itself as free from any attachment, but the passion of the singular subject attaches it to an activity that enables the subject to enjoy itself. Every passion is at once an attachment—either to an object or to an activity. There is no free-floating passion, which helps to distinguish the singularity associated with passion from the typical notion of individuality.

Liberal philosophy asserts the independence of the individual from its environment. The individual, according to this line of thought, exists initially as an isolated monad that subsequently enters into social relations. In his *Second Treatise of Government,* John Locke provides the canonical definition of this conception of individualism. He writes, "Though the Earth, and all inferior Creatures be common to all Men, yet every Man has a *Property* in his own *Person.* This no Body has any Right to but himself" (287). For Locke, individuals exist distinctly from the social order and have a form of control over themselves that others cannot have. This image of an exclusive self-possession implicates the concept of individuality in capitalist relations of production. The category of the individual is the cornerstone of liberal political philosophy.

Though Lee's films that focus on singularity tend to be less explicitly political than his other films, singularity is a political category. The singularity of the subject provides the basis for all capacity for resistance and revolutionary change because it attests to what the ruling order cannot include. Singularity resists the hail of ideology through an excessive attachment that ideology cannot incorporate. Even if a figure of authority demands this attachment, the subject asserts its singularity insofar as it displays more passion than the authority demands, and this excess disturbs the order in which it exists. In contrast to individuality, singularity never fits comfortably within the ruling order.

In Lee's films, characters often display an excessive attachment to their craft, like Jesus Shuttlesworth (Ray Allen) in *He Got Game*, or to their art, like Bleek Gilliam (Denzel Washington) in *Mo' Better Blues*. In each case, the craft or art has a sublime status for the subject and outweighs everything else within the diegetic world. These characters overly commit themselves to what they do. These excessive attachments provide enjoyment for them and for the spectator, but they also serve to free the characters from their different social environments. For Lee, passionate attachment is the basis for emancipation, which is why he spends so much time in his films addressing it.

The idea of a passionate attachment suggests subjection to an external force rather than freedom, and this is exactly how Judith Butler theorizes it. According to Butler, subjection to structures of power operates through the passionate attachments of those subjected. As she notes in *The Psychic Life of Power*, "There is no formation of the subject without a passionate attachment to subjection" (67). Butler views this passionate attachment as the key to the power that power has: subjects don't simply endure their subjection but actually enjoy it, which makes breaking from the grip of power all the more difficult. But in many of Lee's films, passionate attachment takes on a different political weight. Rather than ensconcing subjects more fully within the domain of power structures, it provides a path of emancipation. The subject experiences the passionate attachment as a burden that appears inescapable, but this burden frees the subject from the constraints of its social world.

In his straightforwardly political films, Lee demonstrates an awareness of how excess can attach subjects to their position within the social world in the way that Butler describes. Oftentimes in his films, for instance, the passionate attachment to one's own social identity includes the hatred of other identities. *Do the Right Thing* and *Bamboozled* depict characters passionately attached to their subjection to a social identity and to the enjoyment that this identity provides. Even as the pizzeria owner Sal (Danny Aiello) expresses fondness for the black neighborhood that houses his restaurant, and even as he displays kindness toward certain members of his clientele, he resorts to the word "nigger" when confronted with a tense situation. This attachment to the racism inhering in the social identity of a white American man becomes apparent in *Do the Right Thing*, and it prevents Sal from seeing the reality of the racial dynamic between his restaurant and the neighborhood. This passionate attachment functions as the trigger for the death of Radio Raheem (Bill Nunn) at the hands of the New York City police, which occurs because Sal wildly overreacts to the actions of Radio Raheem and Buggin' Out (Giancarlo Esposito). But in his less straightforwardly political films, Lee shows the other side of the passionate attachment. Here, excess functions as the source of the subject's singularity, not what ties the subject to its symbolic identity.

When examining the entirety of Lee's filmic output, it is as if the explicitly political films are in a dialogue with the less explicitly political ones. The former show what results when subjects fail to embrace the excessiveness of subjectivity present in the latter. One succumbs to the lure of racism, for instance, when one fails to enjoy one's excessive singularity. Excess is the path to freedom, but it leads to imprisonment in one's social identity at the moment when one fails to embrace it fully. The singular subject, as Lee depicts it in his films, thus has a political charge, even when it does not embark on any political project. The betrayal of singularity leaves one always searching for the passion that one has missed. The subject that betrays its singularity becomes an individual and finds itself in the ideological net of identity.

The subject's passionate attachment alienates it from the demands of the social order, whatever these demands might be. The point, as Lee shows, is not defying a certain set of oppressive social demands but holding fast to one's passionate attachment. Excess inheres in this attachment rather than in the specific norms that one defies. The subject immersed in its passionate attachment expresses a radical indifference to such norms, and this indifference allows the subject to sustain its singularity against the pressure of ideology. Though the social norms shift over Lee's films (and over time), what doesn't shift—what is not reducible to temporality or historical context—is the passionate attachment itself that constitutes the subject's singularity.

Singularity finds its ultimate expression in Lee's work in one of his critically dismissed and least popular films, *Mo' Better Blues*. Here, Lee reveals how singularity develops out of an excessive passion that disrupts interpersonal relations, the social order, and even the psychic health of the subject itself. But at the same time, this excessive passion provides a source of sublime enjoyment for the subject and defines who that subject is. The subject's singularity, as *Mo' Better Blues* depicts it, does not exist deep within the person but on the outside, in an object or act that the subject takes up. This is the crucial way in which Lee distinguishes singularity from individuality—what doesn't fit within the social order (subjectivity) from what does (symbolic identity). In the case of Bleek Gilliam, the prized object is the trumpet. The entire film focuses on the trumpet and Bleek's passionate attachment to it, an attachment that becomes evident even during the opening credits. As the credits come on the screen, the camera moves along the trumpet and includes a close-up of Bleek's lips, which make his playing possible and link him to his object.

After the credit sequence, the film opens in 1969, when Bleek is a young boy practicing the trumpet. Neighborhood children come to his window and ask him to come out to play, but Bleek's mother refuses to allow this. He tells her, "I'm sick and tired of the trumpet. I hate the trumpet." In response, his mother commands him to play the scales. We see a close-up of Bleek's mouth on the trumpet as he obeys, and then a match cut to an older Bleek playing at a club illustrates that he has continued his devotion to the trumpet. Lee includes this shot of Bleek's childhood to demystify his attachment to the trumpet. The attachment develops through years of practice, not through an innate ability, and it

Bleek forced to practice as a young boy
in *Mo' Better Blues.*

is an attachment that Bleek suffers. The trumpet defines him and provides enjoyment for him, but it also brings him great suffering. In fact, the suffering that his attachment to the trumpet causes leads Bleek to not demand such an attachment from his son at the end of the film.

The film's final scene reprises the opening and even repeats the same dialogue, but in this instance, Bleek and his spouse Indigo (Joie Lee) are demanding trumpet practice from their own son, Miles (Zakee Howze). The film emphasizes the repetition further through using the same actor to play Miles who earlier played the young Bleek. But in this scene, Bleek allows his son to abandon the trumpet and play with his friends. Bleek recognizes how much he suffered his attachment to the trumpet, and he wants his son to live free of this. Despite this concluding gesture, and despite its depiction of the damage that results, *Mo' Better Blues* emphasizes that excessive attachment is the source of the subject's singularity and of its capacity to enjoy. The disruptiveness of this singularity is the indication of its status outside the conventions of the social order.

Though the film ends with Bleek's capitulation to social norms, it does not present this capitulation as an ideal. In his account of the symbolic role of the trumpet in the film entitled "Signifyin(g) the Phallus," Krin Gabbard correctly apprehends the fundamental opposition that the ending demonstrates. He notes, "In spite of his public statements that *Mo' Better Blues* would correct the myth of the doomed jazz artist presented in *Bird* and *Round Midnight,* Spike Lee has made another film about a self-destructive jazz musician. The hero is not a drug addict or an alcoholic, but he can only be saved by abandoning jazz. Once he renounces the music, the film suggests, his masculinity is restored as he ascends to the role of strong father" (53–54). Gabbard recognizes that the subject excessively committed to the trumpet cannot function in the role of the father, but his interpretation of the film's conclusion as a salvation doesn't do justice to the enjoyment that Bleek derives from his trumpet playing. This enjoyment destroys his ability to have typical social relations and to exist within prevailing social norms, but it also gives him a singularity that others do not readily evince. In this sense, Lee's film celebrates Bleek as a musician, even as he displays the costs of his excessive commitment.

The film makes this point earlier as well, when Bleek loses his ability to play the trumpet. After his friend and manager, Giant (Spike Lee), becomes indebted to the local bookie, Petey (Ruben Blades), Petey sends two enforcers to beat up Giant. As they do so, Bleek intervenes, and one of the men, Madlock (Samuel L. Jackson), hits Bleek across the face with Bleek's trumpet. This blow damages his lips and leaves him unable to play. After a failed comeback attempt a year later, Bleek returns to his former lover Indigo and begs for her to take him back. After some resistance, she agrees, and they later marry. The timing of this act is paramount. It is only after Bleek can no longer play the trumpet that he can settle into a relationship with Indigo. Prior to his injury, he had been involved with both Indigo and Clarke (Cynda Williams), and he had refused to devote himself to either of them. But without his attachment to the trumpet, the socially accepted relationship becomes feasible.

Lee illustrates the disruptiveness of Bleek's excessive commitment to the trumpet early in the film. In a montage sequence, Bleek lovingly assembles his trumpet before practicing. As he practices in his apartment, Clarke interrupts him by ringing the buzzer downstairs. Though he lets her in, he upbraids her for intruding on his practice time. He says to her, "I know what I want, my music. Everything else is secondary." The film supports this idea through the visuals at this point. As they talk, we see Clarke out of focus in the left foreground and Bleek

After having his lips damaged in a fight, Bleek loses his ability to play the trumpet in *Mo' Better Blues*.

in focus in the right background. Their failure to relate here manifests itself through this disjuncture in the image. Later in the scene when they do have sex, Bleek strokes her body with his trumpet, so that the object comes between them even at the most intimate moment. For Bleek, sex cannot provide the enjoyment that he finds in his excessive attachment to the trumpet.

The film contrasts Bleek's excess not only with the women who want a stable relationship with him but with all the other characters as well. The members of Bleek's band—Shadow Henderson (Wesley Snipes), Left Hand Lacey (Giancarlo Esposito), Rhythm Jones (Jeff "Tain" Watts), and Bottom Hammer (Bill Nunn)—all love playing music, but they integrate this love into a balanced life. For instance, Lacey can have a love affair with Jeanne (Linda Hawkins) that disrupts his participation in the band, and Shadow, when he forms his own band after Bleek's injury, can perform with and carry on a relationship with Clarke, which Bleek was incapable of doing. But the most dramatic contrast with Bleek involves the owners of the club where he performs, the Flatbush brothers, Moe (John Turturro) and Josh (Nicholas Turturro).

Whereas Bleek has a singularity that exceeds all calculation, Moe and Josh commit themselves wholly to the world of exchange. Their association with money making brought charges of anti-Semitism against Lee for his depiction of them as Jewish. Because he is a filmmaker of excess, Lee always flirts with stereotypical depictions, and these stereotypes most often involve black characters. (Almost the only black characters who appear in *Summer of Sam*, for instance, are looters who take advantage of a blackout.) The fact that the characters associated with pure money making and the destruction of singularity in *Mo' Better Blues* are Jewish represents a point where Lee simply takes over the classic image of capitalism run amok. The problem isn't with the role that Moe and Josh play in the film but the stereotypical association of Jewishness with the pure logic of capitalism. The function of Moe and Josh in *Mo' Better Blues* is to represent the logic of calculation, in which every apparent singularity can be reduced to a quantity exchangeable with other quantities, and Lee's film clearly adopts a critical attitude toward this reduction.

The first scene involving Moe and Josh appears completely out of context and doesn't present them as the owners of the club where Bleek and his group perform. Instead, it serves as a thematic counterpoint to Bleek's singularity. Lee sets up the appearance of the brothers with two scenes that reveal Bleek's excess and demonstrate what the excess opposes. In the first, we see Clarke and Bleek in a romantic scene that concludes when Clarke bites Bleek's lip. Though she means this as a playful and even sexual gesture, Bleek becomes enraged because she threatens his ability to play the trumpet, which means more to him than his relationship with her. The scene concludes with a close-up of Bleek's lips in the mirror, which lifts his excessive commitment to his music out of the environment and depicts it in isolation.

After Clarke threatens Bleek's singularity, the film cuts to Giant betting on baseball games with his bookie Petey. This represents another depiction of singularity and a move away from it at the same time. Giant's addiction to gambling parallels Bleek's commitment to the trumpet. Both characters pursue their passion excessively and without regard for the damage that it might cause themselves or others; this is what gives the passion its value. But Giant's passion is wholly different from Bleek's as well. The problem isn't that Giant pursues an illegal activity while Bleek engages in a legal one—gambling with a bookie versus playing the trumpet—but that Giant's passion has as its goal the accumulation of money. He subordinates his passion to a monetary calculus, which is exactly what Bleek refuses to do. He will not cater to demands for a more popular type of music or use his trumpet playing as a vehicle for money making. He is paid to play the trumpet, but the pay remains secondary to the trumpet for him, while for Giant, making money from gambling is paramount.

After the scene with Giant and the bookie, the film cuts to the first scene of the Flatbush brothers. In their office, Josh sits in front of the computer screen calculating their finances while Moe stands beside him. Here, the singularity that Bleek evinces and that Giant partakes in completely disappears. Even more than Giant, the Flatbush brothers devote themselves entirely to money making and to numbers. Throughout the scene, the brothers offer a panegyric not to money but to numbers, and the scene concludes with Moe saying, "Numbers never lie." Numbers dominate the thinking of Moe and Josh because numbers enable them both to flee and to incorporate Bleek's singularity. Through the scenes leading up to this one, the film depicts a gradual turning away from this excessive singularity that Moe's proclamation punctuates.

The role that numbers play in *Mo' Better Blues* is central to the film's philosophical significance and places it in proximity to Alain Badiou's magisterial treatise, *Number and Numbers*. Badiou attests to the contemporary predominance of number, which he associates with the unquestioned acceptance of capitalism as an apparently natural socioeconomic system. He claims, "In our situation, that of Capital, the reign of number is thus the reign of the unthought slavery of numericality itself. Number, which, so it is claimed, underlies everything of value, is in actual fact a proscription against any thinking of number itself. Number operates at that obscure point where the situation constitutes its law; obscure through its being at once sovereign and subtracted from all thought, and even from every investigation that orients itself towards some truth" (213). When we immerse ourselves in number, we abandon truth and singularity. Singularity requires an excess, and number produces a world in which everything fits and succumbs to a preestablished calculus. Capitalism may be conducive to individuality, but it is absolutely antithetical to the discovery of singularity. Moe and Josh Flatbush offer the spectator a vision of our contemporary situation, and Bleek represents the possibility of an excessive alternative.

Nonetheless, Moe and Josh Flatbush have their own form of excess: they devote themselves excessively to the regime of calculation. They are excessive slaves of the number. But this form of excess, like that of the wild speculator on the stock market, forms out of a retreat from the excess of the subject's singularity. It is akin to the excess found in racism insofar as it homogenizes the subject into a social identity rather than separating the subject in its singularity. With the Flatbush brothers, Lee reveals how an excessive devotion to an exclusive social identity results from the refusal of the excess associated with singularity. No one escapes excess, but its political determination changes.

The scene that follows the introduction of Moe and Josh emphasizes the contrast between singularity and belonging to a social identity even further. Bleek comes home to Indigo, who upbraids him for being late and confronts him with the question of losing his capacity for playing. She says, "What would you do, Bleek, if you couldn't play anymore?" Bleek responds, "Probably roll up in the corner and die." He then blows in his mouthpiece and adds, "I'd probably play at my own funeral." Here, the film makes clear that the trumpet not only gives Bleek a singularity

The Flatbush brothers represent the logic
of calculation in *Mo' Better Blues*.

that contrasts with the other characters in the film but gives him a reason
to live. Without the enjoyment that trumpet playing provides, life would
be completely empty for Bleek. Though playing the trumpet is just an
activity like any other, Bleek invests it with a sublime importance that
enables it to create value for him.

In his *Seminar VII* entitled *The Ethics of Psychoanalysis,* Jacques
Lacan alters Sigmund Freud's famous definition of sublimation as the
discharge of a libidinal drive through a nonlibidinal act. For Lacan, sublimation occurs at the very core of the drive and produces the subject's
passionate attachment to an object. Through sublimation, an ordinary
object, like a trumpet, becomes charged with a libidinal force that enables it to function as the source of the subject's passion. Or, as Lacan
puts it, "The most general formula that I can give you of sublimation is
the following: it raises an object . . . to the dignity of the Thing" (112).
Sublimation permits us to enjoy an everyday object as if it were transcendent. This is what occurs with Bleek and what doesn't occur with
the Flatbush brothers. While they treat all objects as interchangeable
numbers, Bleek separates one object and transforms it into his thing
through an act of sublimation. He can thus enjoy in a way that others
cannot, and Lee's film is both a celebration of this passion and an il-
lustration of its social and psychic costs.

No one would contend that *Mo' Better Blues* is Lee's masterpiece, but it does provide a clearer matrix of his filmmaking project than any of his other works. In this film, Lee contrasts excess with the domain of calculation and illustrates the passion that excess provides without obscuring the havoc and destruction that it wreaks. The close-ups of Bleek's lips as he plays and the slow traveling shots along the trumpet emphasize the sublimity of the object and its role as a source of value for Bleek. But the trumpet is also the weapon used against Bleek that renders him incapable of playing anymore. Our excessive singularity is always tenuous, and it even tends to undermine itself. But it is only in the act of adhering to this excess that we can find the sublimity that enables us to escape the oppressiveness of our environment.

Though the early *Mo' Better Blues* offers the foremost instance of singularity in Lee's cinema, the later *She Hate Me* illustrates the political and socioeconomic consequences of rejecting singularity more clearly than in any of Lee's other films. The film relates the fall of the pharmaceutical executive Jack Armstrong (Anthony Mackie), who decides to inform the authorities about improprieties at his company, Progeia, which is headed by the corrupt Leland Powell (Woody Harrelson). Though Leland and Margo (Ellen Barkin), another executive at the company, try to convince Jack that he belongs to their "family," he becomes a whistleblower after witnessing the suicide of a researcher, his friend Dr. Herman Schiller (David Bennent), and seeing employees shredding records at night in the office. Jack's willingness to separate himself from the company and take a stand against it does not earn him praise but suspicion and enmity. The company turns on him and begins to survey his actions, while the authorities view him as the prime suspect in the scandal (falsified results in the testing of a new anti-AIDS drug). Because Leland blacklists him and later because he is the subject of a public investigation, no one will hire him, and the authorities freeze his assets. His singular act of defying his situation at the company and pointing out the corruption there leaves him isolated and without any resources.

As a result, Jack accepts an offer from his former fiancée Fatima (Kerry Washington) and her girlfriend Alex (Diana Ramirez) to impregnate them so that they can have children. Though Jack doesn't want to sell himself in this way, the response to his whistleblowing leaves him in a vulnerable position without many attractive options. Soon, Jack and

Fatima establish an operation that caters to lesbians who want a child without going through adoption or a sperm bank. Much of the film recounts Jack's sexual interactions with the women. During these interactions, Jack clearly enjoys himself, but he is also having sex simply for the money that it provides. In contrast with the serious opening of the film that deals with suicide and executive malfeasance, the long sequences depicting Jack with the various women are comic. For instance, after a night of sex, Lee shows an animated sequence of Jack's sperm with his face on each swimming toward an egg with the face of the woman. But the arrangement is very lucrative for Jack. He earns ten thousand dollars for each pregnancy, and the number of women who come to him enables him to sustain his former lifestyle.

Much of the negative critical reaction to *She Hate Me* undoubtedly stems from the disparate tone in the sequences involving the pharmaceutical company and those involving Jack's pregnancy operation. As with other Spike Lee films, the work appears to suffer from incoherence. But here the contrast elucidates a specific idea about singularity. When no one embraces Jack for taking the singular stand and confronting his company, he turns to commodifying himself. Whereas *Mo' Better Blues* contrasts the singularity of Bleek with the homogeneous numbers of the Flatbush brothers, here the contrast plays itself out in an individual character. The failure of the other characters to recognize Jack's singularity leads directly to him abandoning that singularity through a prostitution-like scheme, which the film depicts critically. Our psychic investment in capitalism and its demand for a form of universalized prostitution (selling one's time) arises, Lee's film suggests, through the act of turning away from singularity.

Singularity leaves one, like Jack, on the outside. The singular subject betrays the community or even the family that would incorporate it, but this betrayal contains the essence of its singularity. At the end of the film, before a congressional hearing, Jack reaffirms his commitment to singularity even as it results in a contempt charge. To the committee, he proclaims, "I am Frank Wills." In this act, he identifies himself with the Watergate guard, Frank Wills (Chiwetel Ejiofor), who stopped the burglary and changed the course of the nation. Like Jack, Wills received punishment rather than acclaim for his act, and as Jack's father Geronimo (Jim Brown) explains the story of Frank Wills to him, the film cuts to an imaginary scene that illuminates the difference between those in power who perpetuate crimes and those who expose them.

In this scene, multiple cars surround Wills in the parking garage of the Watergate, and men with guns jump out of each car. Even though Wills is the security guard who has reported the break-in, he finds himself under attack. Each man identifies himself—John Dean, John Erlichman, H. R. Haldeman, G. Gordon Liddy, Jeb Stuart Magruder, and Richard Nixon himself—and announces the social and financial success that they have attained despite their involvement in the Watergate crimes. Even Oliver North drives up in a jeep, and this occasions a wild celebration with the men shooting their guns into the air. They belong to the collective, and the collective protects them. But the collective casts Wills aside because he insists on violating its pact of the repression of all singularity.

By identifying himself with Frank Wills and other whistleblowers, Jack returns from the self-commodication of the pregnancy business and regains the singularity that he had abandoned. He also indicates how a bond can develop among singular subjects, a bond that doesn't involve any constitutive exclusion (like social bonds do). Through this trajectory, *She Hate Me* details exactly what is at stake in our relation to excessive singularity. If we fail to embrace this singularity, our excess doesn't simply disappear. Instead, it manifests itself most often today in our attachment to making money. The opening credits projected over close-ups of various denominations of American currency further underlines this point. The transformation of money into a fetish object (which is what occurs during the credit sequence) is the result of the abandonment of an excessive singularity, a singularity that always disturbs the social order in which it exists.

Excessive singularity is the overriding concern of Lee's cinema. Singularity matters because it is the point from which all critique of ideology emanates. Without singularity, there is only the blind functioning of the social structure. The excessive social ills that Lee diagnoses arise through the repression of this singular excess, which is why he occupies himself with it from his very first feature. This film sets the stage for everything that follows by showing how excess functions as the source of enjoyment and desirability. The titular character and protagonist of *She's Gotta Have It*, Nola Darling, refuses to accept the demands of monogamy that the culture and her three boyfriends attempt to place

Nola Darling exceeds the constraints of monogamy in *She's Gotta Have It*.

on her. Her excessive enjoyment manifests itself in her three very different partners, all of whom know of the existence of the other. Rather than hide her nonmonogamous enjoyment, Nola parades it, and Lee's first film celebrates her for this. Her rejection of cultural constraints and embrace of her own enjoyment make her a singular subject, and this arouses the desire of other characters in the film and the spectator.

After some external shots of New York City, *She's Gotta Have It* opens with a long shot of Nola sleeping in her apartment. The camera slowly tracks toward her as she wakes up and comes out from under the blankets. Nola then begins a direct address to the camera in which she talks about her love of sex. This shot of Nola in her bed and of her confession structures the film, which concludes with a return to the same image of Nola in bed. All the events that occur between these two images are in response to the intensity of Nola's passion and the singularity that this passion announces.

Though the film lacks much narrative development, it does show three men and three women responding to Nola. The three men each try to eliminate Nola's enjoyment of sex and to prod her into a monogamous relationship with them. As the film depicts it, the men exist only in relation to Nola: we don't see anything about their lives apart from how they view her. Even when they appear in the film without Nola, they speak in direct address to the camera about her.

The women in Nola's life have a less pronounced role in the film than the men, but they relate to her in a similar fashion. Opal Gilstrap (Raye Dowell) tries to seduce her into a lesbian relationship that Nola resists. Her former roommate Clorinda Bradford (Joie Lee) moves out because she cannot live with Nola's multiple sexual liaisons. And Dr. Jamison (S. Epatha Merkerson) tries to treat Nola for sex addiction, though Nola abandons the treatment after only one session. Just like the men in Nola's life, the three women find that her sexuality disturbs them and forces them to either flee it or direct it into more acceptable paths. They all fail in their efforts, but the focus of the film is the more pronounced failures of the men.

Critics have taken Lee to task for the depiction of Nola and for the fact that we see her through the lens of male fantasies. William A. Harris provides a representative statement of this position: "Nola is, in fact, a woman in a man's suit, a persona constructed from the male standpoint" (33). In the same vein, Norman Denzin adds, "Nola arouses masochistic and insatiable male sexual fantasies. . . . She is defined solely through her sexuality, which is rooted in her body, but defined in male, heterosexual terms" (107). Nola exists as a threat, not as a potential partner. But this is precisely Lee's point, and the film indicts the men for their failure to accept Nola's singularity rather than indicting her for arousing the men without satisfying them. Though she appears within male fantasies throughout the film, she always exceeds the domain of the fantasy and disrupts its power to render her singularity meaningful for the men.

The failure of the three men to accept Nola on her own terms marks the disruptiveness of her singularity. If Nola easily fit into their definitions of feminine identity, each of them could manage a relationship with her. But her excessive singularity renders such a relationship impossible. Lee reveals this singularity through the failed attempts to contain it. We see how Nola's subjectivity disturbs Jamie Overstreet (Tommy Redmond Hicks), Greer Childs (John Canada Terrell), and Mars Blackmon (Spike Lee). Each man proclaims his devotion to Nola and at the same time his inability to endure her sexuality. After trying to call Nola while she is having sex with Mars, Jamie proclaims, "Nola hurt me to the core, but she's gotta

None of the three lovers can contain
Nola in *She's Gotta Have It.*

have it." At this point, Jamie speaks for all three lovers. Nola's singularity drives them to pursue her, but it also bars them from possessing her.

The contrast between Nola's singularity and her three lovers becomes fully apparent when she invites all of them to Thanksgiving dinner at her apartment. Lee shows each man trying to impress her and gain an advantage over the other two. This contrasts with Nola, who doesn't go out of her way to attract their desire. Lee illustrates this contrast formally during the dinner. He alternates between shots from Nola's perspective that show the three men seated at the table and shots of Nola alone at the head of the table. While the men almost always appear as a group in this scene, Nola is isolated, and even though she is at the table with them, she exists apart in her own world. The three men have their respective idiosyncrasies, but they lack the singularity that Nola has, which leads Lee to film them in the way that he does.

The film comes to a crisis point when Jamie, the privileged lover for Nola, can no longer endure her refusal to commit to a monogamous relationship. He begins to date someone else, and when Nola calls him and asks him to see her, he comes to her apartment and rapes her. Jamie rapes Nola from behind as she is bent forward. Lee shoots the sequence from in front of Nola's face, so that we see the look on her face and her revulsion at the behavior of the man she loves. Immediately after the rape, the film cuts to an image that Nola has painted on her apartment wall that resembles Edvard Munch's *The Scream* and suggests the horror of what has happened.

Subsequently, however, Nola continues to desire Jamie and calls the incident a "near-rape" rather than an actual rape. This leads feminist interpreters to criticize Lee for making light of violence toward women. The most prominent of these is bell hooks, who claims that this scene promulgates the idea that "rape is an effective means of patriarchal control" and "suggests to black females, and all females, that being sexually assertive will lead to rejection and punishment" (233). Though Lee himself has accepted some of the criticism of this scene (claiming in an interview with George Khoury, "The only thing I would like to do over is that rape scene in *She's Gotta Have It*" [152]), it actually reveals rape occurring as a response to the failure of patriarchal control rather than as a "means of patriarchal control." Jamie rapes Nola because he can't reduce her singularity to the prescribed role that he envisions for her, and Lee's depiction of the rape scene highlights his sense of failure.

While he rapes Nola, Jamie demands that she proclaim his ownership over her sexuality. He asks her—and this question provides the title for hooks's essay on the film—"Whose pussy is this?" Nola finally responds, "Yours." For hooks, this marks a capitulation to patriarchal power, but the film shows that the question itself emerges not out of Jamie's strength but out of his complete weakness in the face of Nola's singularity. The question and forced response are an attempt to contain this singularity, and they testify to the power of Nola's singularity rather than to the power of patriarchy. Though Nola goes back to Jamie after the rape and abandons her other lovers, the way that she does so reveals that his patriarchal power remains completely feckless in relation to her. She tells him that she will devote herself to him but at the same time will commit herself to celibacy.

When Jamie finally has her, she abandons the sexuality that he desires in her. Then, in the film's epilogue, Nola speaks to the camera and says that she soon gave up Jamie and her vow of celibacy. Though she does not call the police or refuse to see Jamie immediately after the rape, she does avow his inability to domesticate the singularity of her subjectivity. Lee includes the rape sequence not to punish Nola for her sexuality but to reveal the inability of even the understanding man—Jamie appears much more sympathetic than Greer or Mars—to deal with the trauma of singularity, especially when it manifests itself in female sexuality. Singularity is traumatic insofar as it doesn't fit within the forms of social identity with which we typically interact. It disrupts our conventional responses, just like Nola disrupts the conventional demand for a monogamous partner.

Though one might not go so far as to claim that *She's Gotta Have It* is a feminist film, it is safe to say that it functions as a critique of patriarchal sexual relations and a revelation of patriarchy's powerlessness when confronted with a woman's singularity. In this film, Lee links the exploration of singularity to a political project. We see the holes within patriarchal domination when we see Nola's singularity. The latter holds the key to the confrontation with the former, though this singularity doesn't simply disturb the male characters in the film. Lee shows it disturbing a lesbian character (which bespeaks his refusal to romanticize lesbian romance), and the response of various interpreters reveals that it discomfits them as well.

The singularity of Nola's excessive enjoyment bothers not only the characters within the filmic diegesis but also critics watching the film. Karen Hoffman laments Nola's inability to take up any clear social identity and to clarify her mode of enjoying. Hoffman writes, "The character of Nola seems to be undefined. It might be true that she's gotta have it, but it's never really clear who Nola is, exactly what she wants, or how she wants it" (111). This complaint about the characterization of Nola identifies what stands out about her—her inability to occupy fully any identity—but it fails to recognize that this is the key to her singularity as a figure. When one can be defined and it is clear who one is, this implies an existence within the confines of the social structure and its elimination of the subject's singularity. The "undefined" nature of Nola's character testifies to her singular status, not to her failure as a feminist icon.

Though *She's Gotta Have It* details nothing but failures in Nola's relationships with other people, these failures are instructive. None of the men in the film can have a relationship with Nola because none of them can accept her singularity. But this singularity is simultaneously what draws them to her. They thus can't accept the trauma of their own desire, and the film exposes this inability not only to indict the male response to Nola (though it does do this very clearly) and to highlight her excess; it also suggests that one must embrace this excess without trying to diminish it. Though Jamie's rape is the most shocking retreat from Nola's singularity, even Nola attempts to distance herself from it when she returns to Jamie and embarks on a project of monogamy. If singularity is inextricable from our passion, then abandoning it for the sake of social recognition or a romantic attachment is unthinkable, which is why Nola must abandon her attempt at monogamy at the end of the film. We can lose our singularity amid the confines of social demands and identities that we take up, and this will enable us to fit in. But the cost will be our capacity for passion, which derives from our failure to embody proffered social identities rather than our capacity for doing so.

After the depiction of Nola Darling, Lee depicts other forms of excessive enjoyment, including the attachment of Jesus Shuttlesworth (Ray Allen) to the game of basketball in *He Got Game*. As with Bleek and Nola, the excess troubles the character's ability to interact with other characters and at times damages the character's self-interest. But Lee nonetheless shows that the excess defines the singularity of each character. Without excess, there would be no character at all.

The singularity of the hero of *He Got Game* stems directly from his ability to play basketball. Though the film presents basketball as an activity that unites all types of Americans, Jesus Shuttlesworth stands out from the crowd for his unsurpassed capacity to excel in all aspects of the game. The film's opening credit sequence expresses the universality of the game through a montage of people of all races playing basketball in various milieus, from the inner-city playground to the country backyard. While this visual montage goes on, the audio track utilizes the quintessentially American music of the composer Aaron Copland. As Krin Gabbard points out in his essay on the film's use of music, "Spike Lee has made a powerful statement by combining images of young black men playing basketball with music written by the one composer in the classical tradition considered by many to be 'the most American'" (371). Copland's music, which provides most of the soundtrack for the film, bespeaks the same universality in an American context that basketball does. The images that Lee chooses in the introduction are both urban and rural, white and black, and they attempt to represent a common thread that unites these disparate regions and groups, just as Copland's music does. As a result, the images and the music of the opening fit together perfectly.

In one sense, *He Got Game* functions as a celebration of the enjoyment of basketball. Both the common players and the superstar are able to enjoy themselves through basketball in a way that they otherwise wouldn't be able to do. Even though it is just a game, basketball acquires a sublime status in the film, and Lee is not critical of this. He does not indict the United States for paying so much attention to basketball while people starve or while the country fights unnecessary wars. The film is not a political critique of basketball's sublimity for those who love it but a thoroughgoing embrace of that sublimity, despite a recognition of its social and psychic costs. As a sublime activity, it has the ability to bring people together and to give their lives a purpose they otherwise wouldn't have.

But the focus of *He Got Game* is not so much on the universality of basketball as an activity. As his name suggests, Jesus Shuttlesworth is not an ordinary character. Though we find out midway through the film that his father named him for the basketball player Earl Monroe (nicknamed "Jesus") rather than for Christ, the link between Jesus Shuttlesworth and salvation is ubiquitous throughout the film. His superior basketball skills are evident during the film's narrative sequences, but the spectator's sense of his otherworldly talent becomes fully affirmed throughout a series of basketball coaches, players, and authorities speaking directly into the camera about Jesus's ability. Lee uses real-life figures in direct address to add weight to their statements and to convince the spectator of Jesus's greatness in a way that no quantity of basketball-playing sequences could do. Jesus has the endorsement of actual great coaches and players, as well as the endorsement of the broadcaster most identified with college basketball at the time, Dick Vitale. The form in which these figures deliver their praise adds to its excess: the direct address to the camera violates the convention of narrative filmmaking and reveals the emphasis that Lee places on form itself. These encomiums create an aura around Jesus that causes him to stand out from all the other characters in the film. He is a character of excess: his basketball skill and his love for the game give him a singularity that is not apparent in anyone else. The subject's singularity, for Lee, is the product of some form of excess, which in the case of Jesus Shuttlesworth is his association with basketball.

The film makes it clear that Jesus's singular basketball skill is the result of the excessive training to which Jake submits him as a young man. This excess begins even before he is born when Jake decides to name his son after Earl Monroe, a New York Knicks basketball player known as "Jesus" for his incredible skill. After his birth, Jake's son undergoes an intensive basketball education. *He Got Game* shows Jake working with Jesus in the evening at the local basketball court, and we see Jake go so far as to berate Jesus for his softness as a player and to push his son to the ground during their practice.

Despite the celebration of basketball that occurs in *He Got Game*, Lee also shows how Jesus suffers his excessive attachment to the game. This suffering linked to basketball is the film's endpoint, its punctuation of a running time devoted to celebrating the game and its art. Lee concludes the film with a turn to fantasy. Though it is actually shot more realistically and with fewer formal flourishes than most of Lee's films, a fantasmatic moment transpires in the final scene that appears to portend a reconciliation between father and son, Jake and Jesus. Back at the prison basketball court where he repetitively shoots baskets, Jake steps across the prison boundary, prompting a guard to warn him to return onto the court. Jake ignores the warning, and it initially seems as if the guard will shoot him. But then Jake heaves the basketball over the prison wall. Jesus, who is shooting alone in the gym at Big State University, sees the basketball that his father has thrown magically appear bounding onto his court. The ball doubly connects the father and son: it is the privileged object that they both have in common, and the father has here repeated the earlier act of the son, who jettisoned the ball from the playground court after he grew weary of his father's overwhelming pressure on him to excel at basketball.

The impossible appearance of the basketball on the Big State court leads the spectator to believe that the film displays the possibility of reconciliation even in the face of incredible wrong (Jake's role in the death of Jesus's mother). This is the interpretation advanced by Krin Gabbard, who notes, "The film is much more about the oedipal reconciliation between father and son than it is about a young man's rise to success in professional athletics" (380). Gabbard's sense that the film's primary concern is the relationship between father and son is insightful, but this relationship is inextricable from their shared commitment to basketball.

The reconciliation between father and son comes from a shared grasp of the suffering that their attachment to basketball imposes on them. Jesus's act of throwing the basketball far off the court and into the night sky does not express a rejection of basketball as such. Though we don't see his childhood past this point, we can safely assume that he continued to play basketball in the path laid down by his father. This training enables him to become the top high-school player in the country during the present time in the film. By jettisoning the basketball, Jesus indicates that the weight of his father's excessive devotion to the game and to his son's performance overwhelms him, and the act even hints at the possibility that Jesus finds his own devotion to the game burdensome. We see Jesus enjoy playing basketball throughout the film, but we also see how much sacrifice this passion requires, not only in terms of training but also in terms of its effect on every relationship that he has. In Jesus's flashback to the evening when he threw the ball away, the cost of the commitment to basketball becomes fully visible.

Up to this point, the spectator knows that Jake is serving a long prison sentence for murder but knows none of the facts surrounding the murder. The flashback, which occurs toward the end of the film, provides enlightenment while displaying how much Jake and Jesus have lost because of their excessive passion for basketball. The conflict between father and son that occurred during their play continues as they come inside for dinner. During the continued confrontation, Jake again pushes Jesus, which causes Martha (Lonette McKee), his mother, to intervene. When she tries to stop Jake's aggressiveness toward his son, Jake pushes her away, and her head slams against the counter. She falls to the ground, and it is clear immediately that the blow kills her. At this moment, it is also clear that Jake's excessive attachment to basketball—his desire to see his son become a great player—produces this result.

The cost of excess in the film is high: Jake loses his freedom and ends up in prison; Martha loses her life; and Jesus loses both his parents. And yet, the devotion to basketball that Jake passes on to Jesus makes Jesus sublime. His achievements on the basketball court are unequaled, and he transforms basketball, in Lee's rendering, into an art form. Because of Jake, Jesus is a figure of excess, but despite its costs, this excess gives him a singularity that the other characters in the film desire.

Jesus's excessive attachment to and skill at basketball presents an opportunity for others. Almost everyone looks to capitalize on Jesus, and the structure of the film highlights this by centering on his decision about where he will play the year after high school. Even those closest to Jesus—like his father (who needs Jesus to go to Big State in order to gain freedom from prison), his Uncle Bubba (Bill Nunn), his girlfriend Lala (Rosario Dawson), and his high-school coach (Arthur J. Nascarella)—want to use him to enrich themselves. Through the depiction of this dynamic, Lee shows the relationship between the subject's excessive singularity and the social world in which the subject exists.

This singularity functions as a threat to everyone else because it signals a form of enjoyment that they lack. No one else can play like Jesus, and thus everyone else wants to become close to him in order to enjoy along with him. By associating with him and capitalizing on his singularity, the others eliminate the threat that this singular enjoyment poses for them. They share in it, and they force it to work for some good (often their own) rather than remaining an end in itself. Lee's film, however, offers a thorough critique of all these attempts to reincorporate Jesus's singularity, and the account of Jesus's final choice reflects this critique.

Though the decision about his future is the event that the entire structure of *He Got Game* leads to and revolves around, Lee does not present the moment of the final decision onscreen. Instead, he plays a game of one-on-one against Jake with the stake that Jesus will go to Big State if he loses but not if he wins. When Jesus wins by a score of 11–5 and the officers take Jake back to prison, it seems as if Jesus will not go to Big State. But the next scene is a press conference in which the high-school coach reads Jesus's statement expressing his intention to go to Big State. As the coach reads the statement publicly, Lee crosscuts to Jesus speaking the same words in private through a direct address to the camera.

The film elides the decision itself and presents it only after Jesus has made it. This formal choice affirms the singularity of Jesus because it testifies to his irreducibility to the world in which he exists. No one within the diegetic reality of the film sees Jesus articulate his choice, and even we as spectators do not see the moment of the choice itself. He constantly insists to everyone who asks that he wants to take his time, but the time itself never arrives. By holding back the decision from the visual field and by locating it outside of what the film shows, Lee emphasizes once again the singularity of Jesus. We cannot know what triggered the decision for Big State because the decision remains an absence within the film's field of signification. The subject's excess creates its singularity, but this singularity can only appear as an absence within signification.

Lee's documentaries devoted to a single individual, like *Jim Brown: All American* and *Kobe Doin' Work*, take the excess of their subject as the point of departure. In the former, Brown's excessive singlemindedness and refusal to give ground function as the central idea of the film. This excess even explains Brown's limitations. When his costar Raquel Welch tries to account for Brown's inability to succeed fully on the screen, she suggests that his refusal to bend to the demands of others compromises his ability to act. In her terms, he is too masculine and too lacking in the feminine side that acting requires. Lee traces this excess from Brown's football career to his time in Hollywood to his years as an activist. In each case, Brown's excessive refusal to acquiesce brings him success and failure, glory on the football field and trouble with the law. Lee chronicles a related dynamic in *Kobe Doin' Work*, though here it is Kobe Bryant's excessive effort that marks his singularity.

The singularity of a subject emerges most clearly in Lee's films through his signature shot, which first appears in *Mo' Better Blues*: a tracking shot (usually a reverse tracking shot) that shows a character moving in contrast to the background but without walking or running. The movement of the character follows the movement of the tracking camera, and Lee does this by placing the character on the dolly with the camera. In an interview with Erich Leon Harris, he describes how he creates the shot: "To get that shot you have to lay dolly tracks. Then you put the camera on the dolly. Then you put the actors on the dolly also. Then you move the dolly along" (131). The effect is similar to the trombone shot or dolly zoom that Steven Spielberg famously used in *Jaws* (1975), when Police Chief Martin Brody (Roy Scheider) reacts to a shark attack on the beach. Spielberg tracks back with the camera while zooming in toward Brody. Lee typically tracks back without zooming but instead places the actor on the tracking dolly, which produces movement without any apparent reason for the movement. This shot appears in almost all of Lee's later fiction films, and his version of the shot violates the conventions of verisimilitude even more than Spielberg's. Characters appear as if they are magically floating across the ground or through the air, radically separated from their environment.

None of Lee's formal idiosyncrasies creates as much controversy as this shot. Critics object not only to its use—which is bad enough—but to its excessive use. It often appears multiple times in his films, and the violation of the conventions of verisimilitude becomes more apparent with each use. Bert Cardullo exemplifies this line of critique. He says, "I can only conclude that [Lee's] time spent in film school (at New York University) has addicted him to cinematic trickery, to the legerdemain of the studio over the reality of the street. How else can one explain his outrageous use—twice!—of a traveling matte behind two characters in conversation [in *Jungle Fever*], which creates the illusion that they are taking a walk when in fact they're standing still?" (643). Cardullo experiences Lee's dolly shot as a violation of "the reality of the street," and this objection is essentially correct. Cardullo indicts Lee for succeeding at the fundamental idea that animates his filmmaking: the excessive singularity of the subject is not reducible to the social reality out of which this subject emerges. The dolly shot violently breaks from the reality of the street to show that this reality is not fully determinative for the subject in a way that verisimilitude cannot relay.

The dolly shot in *Malcolm X*
just before Malcolm's death.

Through this type of shot, Lee indicates the subject's relationship to its environment, its status as an excess relative to the place it occupies. Lee is not simply playing a formal game by repeatedly introducing this shot but instead punctuating his cinema's most significant philosophical idea. Here, Lee's films perform a formal operation with an apparent gimmick in the manner of Hitchcock's. The Hitchcock cameo has the same status for critics and fans as Lee's dolly shot: critics tend to mock it, while fans revere it. Both are instances of excess. But as Raymond Bellour points out, even this seemingly nonsensical nod to the director's fans demands interpretation. For Bellour, it becomes the key to understanding the role of fantasy in Hitchcock's films. He notes, "[Hitchcock's] appearances occur, more and more frequently, at that point in the chain of events where what could be called the film wish is condensed. It is an authorial signature, of course, but an exaggerated one that punctuates the logical unfolding of the fantasy originating in the conditions of enunciation. This operation is similar to that of the Freudian pun" (224). Unlike other critics, who view the cameo as an insignificant excess in the Hitchcock film, Bellour attempts to interpret it. He grasps that this excess provides the key to Hitchcock's filmic universe. This is also the case with Spike Lee's signature dolly shot.

Just as Hitchcock's excessive cameos point to the central fantasy of his films, Lee's dolly shot identifies his overarching concern with the singularity of the subject. This singularity proceeds with an excessive relationship to its environment. Though Lee often shows how a social environment can determine those who inhabit it, he refuses to remain within a vision of social determinism. To do so would be to abandon the possibility for political agency that animates his filmic vision. The excessive subject is an incipiently political subject, and Lee sees no better way of communicating this excess than the repetition of the dolly shot.

The excessive status of the dolly shot leads Jerold Abrams to label it "sublime." In the experience of the sublime, the subject escapes its immersion in the world and transcends the limits associated with the world. Abrams notes, "The signature shot is an image of what it is like to experience the sublime from the inside. It portrays the experience of aesthetic and emotional transcendence and elevation, a sense that one is beyond one's own limitations and beyond all human limitations"

(197–98). The dolly shot depicts a character transcending the limitations of the filmic world, and at the same time, it forces spectators into the same movement of transcendence. It dislocates them from the comfortable position that the spectator usually inhabits. The result is not Brecht's alienation effect, however. The spectator isn't thrust out of the filmic world back into an awareness of the world of the theater itself. Instead, the confrontation with the dolly shot allows a transcendence of the filmic world and that of the theater. Through this shot, our capacity for transcending our place becomes evident.

When the subject exceeds its place, it challenges the dictates of ideology and the imperatives of the ruling class. Alain Badiou makes this clear in his *Theory of the Subject*, where he points out, "A ruling class is the guardian of the place" (184). By guarding place and keeping subjects in their proper place, ideology aims at preventing any hiccup in its dictates and envisions what Badiou calls "the blockage of interruption" (184). Simply by depicting singular subjects who break from their place, Lee implicitly articulates a political vision that begins by vitiating the communal bond, which is always an ideological bond. Politics, as Lee's films conceive it, requires the interruption of the community and the assertion of singularity. This is most evident in Lee's unusual dolly shot.

Though Lee uses this shot in almost every film, he uses it at two points in *Inside Man* in a way that directly reveals its significance for him. The first occurs when the bank robber Dalton Russell (Clive Owen) describes the cooperation with the Nazis during World War II of the bank founder, Arthur Case (Christopher Plummer). As Russell talks in the bank with Case's emissary, Madeline White (Jodie Foster), Lee cuts to a tracking shot in which Case is sitting at his desk and impossibly moving forward (with the desk) while the background recedes. Then the film cuts 180 degrees to a shot from Case's perspective moving toward the humanitarian awards sitting on a table on his office. While we see these images, Russell says, "He used his position with the Nazis to enrich himself, while all around him people were being stripped of everything they owned." This sequence reveals that despite all Case's subsequent humanitarian activity, what defines him as a character—what gives him his singularity—is his act of profiteering on the Holocaust. Nothing can remove this singularity, not simply because of the horror of the act itself but because he continues to enjoy the monetary gains from it. He used what Russell calls the "blood money" to open the bank that Russell robs, and the diamonds that Russell steals are the direct result of Case's complicity with the Nazi extermination.

Later in the film, Lee again employs his signature dolly shot. After Russell stages the fake execution of a hostage, Detective Keith Frazer (Denzel Washington), the chief hostage negotiator, explodes. He charges out of the police command unit, and the film shows him moving rapidly toward the bank. But Frazer is not running; he is moving on the dolly of a fast reverse tracking shot. For approximately five seconds, we see Frazer magically transported against a receding background of buildings and other police officers. Lee opts for the signature dolly shot here because Frazer's anger separates him from his context. Though his anger is justified (unlike Case's profiteering on the Holocaust), it nonetheless exceeds the context in which he is located. He can no longer act in the objective capacity of the negotiator but now has a passionate investment in the situation. His singularity at this moment comes to the fore.

There is a philosophical difference between particularity and singularity that Lee's dolly shot recognizes. The particular qualities of one's identity derive from the environment or context out of which one emerges. One is Muslim or Catholic, black or white, straight or gay, Italian or Algerian, rich or poor, and so on. Particularity can be enumerated and delineated. It also fails to create distinctiveness. One particular identity can simply be the same as another, as long as each embodies the same qualities. With singularity, the case is altogether different. Singularity stems from the

Keith Frazer transcends his
context in *Inside Man*.

subject's failure to embody fully the various identities given to it by the cultural context.

Whereas people gain their particularity from the various communities to which they belong, their singularity constantly provides a problem for those communities. As the Marxist thinker Kojin Karatani puts it in *Architecture as Metaphor*, "singularity—as distinct from a particularity—cannot be reduced to a bundle of sets, to any generality. Singularity, contrary to the nuances it may convey, has nothing to do with bourgeois individualism; paradoxically enough, singularity is inseparable from society, from being 'in between' communities" (152). Singularity testifies to our failure to belong or to fit in, and this failure is evident throughout Lee's films, but nowhere more clearly than in his singular dolly shot. In fact, the shot itself formally performs the singularity that it depicts. Because it looks so unusual and distinctive, no other director would think to employ it. This type of dolly shot thus testifies to Lee's own singularity as a filmmaker. When we see it, we know that we are watching a Spike Lee film.

While Lee uses the distinctive dolly shot to mark how a subject exceeds its environment, he employs a more traditional shot to show the opposite—the subject belonging to its context and acting within that context. To show this, Lee shoots a 360-degree tracking shot, which has the opposite effect of his dolly shot. The 360-degree tracking shot often has a vertiginous effect, but it always depicts characters within their environment rather than apart from it. The shot emphasizes the background in relation to the characters.

The 360-degree tracking shot also occurs in *Inside Man*, and Lee turns to it when the power broker Madeline White meets with the New York City mayor (Peter Kybart) to force her way into the hostage negotiations and protect the secrets of Arthur Case, who has hired her. White works as a functionary of power and wants to sustain the workings of those in power. Consequently, there is no singularity in this scene, just the functioning of the environment itself and its determination. When White and the mayor enter a private room to discuss her proposal (which she blackmails the mayor into accepting), the camera moves around them as they talk so that their relationship to the room becomes fully apparent. The nefarious machinations of power, Lee implies, occur within the social context and fail to break from it. Through these two very different types

The 360-degree tracking shot in *Inside Man*.

of shots, the difference between singularity and particularity becomes evident on the level of form.

Driven by Fantasy

The singularity of the subjects that appear in Lee's films is located in their mode of passion, an excess that alienates them from the environment in which they exist. But the excessive dimension of passion becomes visible through the realm of fantasy, and many of Lee's films explore the determinative role that fantasy plays in structuring our subjectivity. Lee forces the spectator to confront the constitutive role of fantasy in producing the subject itself. We discover the mode of enjoyment that produces our singularity through the turn to fantasy or the choice of fantasies. Lee indulges in numerous formal excesses to envision the various fantasies that his characters—and that all subjects—inhabit. Rather than functioning as a respite from the tedium of everyday life, fantasy provides the matrix for the subject's being. The kernel of the subject's fantasy defines what the subject is. Fantasy's excesses inform all of the subject's interactions with other characters and the spectator's interaction with the screen.

Fantasy emerges in response to the dissatisfaction inherent in our social reality. We fantasize a satisfaction that we cannot otherwise attain. But at the same time, fantasy provides our unique perspective on our social reality, the lens through which we can garner enjoyment from the world in which we must exist. Without fantasy, we would live out an existence bereft of any capacity for enjoyment, and we would thus never engage ourselves in the world. As Juan-David Nasio puts it in his psychoanalytic account of fantasy, "The motor of fantasy is a core of enjoyment around which the fantasmatic staging is organized" (44). Though we tend to think of fantasy as a mode of existential retreat, it is also the alibi for engagement in the world. It enlivens our social reality with possibilities for enjoyment that would otherwise be completely absent.

Lee's films explore fantasy through the excesses of editing and mise-en-scène. The montage sequences in *Summer of Sam* and *Bamboozled* indicate that the films have entered into a wholly fantasmatic world where enjoyment dictates the terms of what happens regardless of the exigencies of verisimilitude. In films like *25th Hour* or *Miracle at St. Anna,* the immersion in fantasy occurs through elements of the mise-en-scène—a dramatic change in lighting and setting at the conclusion of *25th Hour* and the unexpected appearance of the benevolent German commander and his gesture of handing Hector (Laz Alonso) a Lugar just before a German soldier can kill him in *Miracle at St. Anna.* These moments that exceed the conventions of realism testify to the power of fantasy in Lee's cinematic worlds. Fantasy doesn't just rescue soldiers on the verge of death but shapes the way that we see the world, and Lee's films force us to avow the power of this fantasmatic distortion not in order to escape from it but in order to embrace it.

The film most overtly devoted to the exploration of fantasy is *Girl 6,* a work in which fantasy so thoroughly predominates the mise-en-scène that there is almost nothing outside of it. Like other Lee films (such as *Inside Man*), *Girl 6* begins with direct address to the camera by the main character. Though it isn't initially obvious through what she says, Girl 6 is auditioning for a role in a film. She attempts to transform herself in this first scene into a fantasy object for the director testing her. Though she ultimately refuses the director's demands (for nudity) and doesn't get the role, the immersion in fantasy characterizes her and the other characters throughout the film.

The most obvious way that Lee reveals the importance of fantasy in the film is through the names of the characters. The main character is known only as Girl 6, and the other women with whom she works at the phone-sex operation are also identified only by their number—like Girl

39 (Debi Mazor), Girl 19 (Dina Pearlman), Girl 42 (Maggie Rush), Girl 4 (Desi Moreno), and Girl 75 (Naomi Campbell). The callers who play major roles in the film, like Bob Regular (Peter Berg), have pseudonyms but not, as far as the spectator knows, actual names. Even Girl 6's ex-husband (Isaiah Washington), who appears frequently in the film, has no name to identify him, and the closing credits list him as "Shoplifter," which is the activity associated with him and not, of course, his name. By refusing to give names to the women who work at the phone-sex operation, Lee thoroughly ensconces them in the fantasy world of phone sex and gives them no identity outside of this world. The fantasy defines their existence within the filmic reality.

The power of the fantasy world created through phone sex comes to take over the entire existence of Girl 6. Unlike the other women working at the phone-sex company, she devotes herself entirely to the fantasy that she creates for the men and for herself. The other women take up hobbies to divert themselves from the fantasies that they're producing: they knit, read, draw, or find some other outlet for their attention. Despite the advice she receives to adopt a diverting hobby, Girl 6 never does. She immerses herself in the fantasy world.

As a result of her total commitment to the fantasy world of phone sex, Girl 6 finds herself increasingly obsessed with the work and the clients. She violates the rules and gives one of her callers, Bob Regular, her home number, and they even set up a meeting. This indicates the extent to which the fantasy life determines her real life, but it also represents an attempt to realize the fantasy, to bring the fantasy into the realm of reality. Lee films the arranged meeting in a way that emphasizes the complete isolation of Girl 6 at this moment. He uses a long tracking shot along the boardwalk where they agree to meet, and the shot passes several empty benches until it arrives at Girl 6 sitting by herself.

After the film depicts her sitting on the bench, it cuts several times to show her looking around for Bob. On each occasion, her face is in focus while the background is blurry. This absence of any depth of field reflects her alienation from the world in which she exists. Girl 6 is alone with her fantasy, and the social reality around her has no connection with this fantasy. Bob never comes, and the fantasy is never realized. Though she exists almost entirely within the fantasy, she cannot simply wish the fantasy into reality. The fantasy removes one from one's world and provides one's enjoyment, but it remains separated from the world and leaves the subject isolated. Any realization of the fantasy would destroy the consistency of the subject's world. If Bob did show up, in other words, the result would be catastrophic.

Even when the fantasy is threatening or potentially dangerous, *Girl 6* makes clear that this separation between fantasy and the world of reality persists. When Girl 6 begins to work at home, a scary caller (Michael Imperioli) verbally assaults her and demands that she say, "I'm not happy because I'm a fuck-slut." As the scary caller interacts with her on the phone, Lee cuts between him and Girl 6, who is moving in one of Lee's typical dolly tracking shots. During some of the crosscuts, Lee uses an anamorphic lens to cause Girl 6 to look squeezed within the frame. These filmic effects express how far the fantasy realm of phone sex removes her from her surrounding world. The scary caller even informs Girl 6 that he knows her real address, and the danger seems quite real. But it amounts to nothing. The fantasy determines the being of Girl 6, but it never realizes itself, even when this realization seems most imminent, as with the scary caller's threat.

The depiction of the danger associated with fantasy becomes most prominent through a news story that Lee intersperses within the narrative surrounding Girl 6. Early in the film, she watches a television news program that discusses a young girl falling down an elevator shaft and becoming critically injured. Just after the news report, Lee cuts to a shot from the perspective of someone falling down a dark elevator shaft. This shot recurs multiple times in the film at the moments when Girl 6's fantasy life seems to become a threat. Before and after the scary caller interacts with her, Lee uses this shot to indicate the danger that fantasy represents.

Despite this depiction of the potential dangers that lie in the realm of fantasy, *Girl 6* is not a warning against delving into fantasy. The controlling idea of the film is that fantasy provides a domain of excess where one organizes one's enjoyment. Fantasy enables Girl 6 not only to earn money but also to find an enjoyment that is otherwise absent in her life. Her relationship with her ex-husband, her only romantic relationship in the film, provides no sexual enjoyment, but her work as a phone-sex operator does. In fact, the only erotic moment with her ex-husband occurs when they playfully act out a phone-sex call during dinner at a restaurant. Though she caters to the fantasies of the male callers, the job also demands that she create her own fantasies as well, and it is her skill at creating and enjoying fantasies that makes her the most popular operator at the company.

The chief critic of the occupation that Girl 6 takes up is her neighbor and friend Jimmy (Spike Lee). He upbraids her for turning to what he calls "phone bone" to support herself. It is tempting for the spectator to identify Jimmy as a point of identification outside of Girl 6's fantasy world from which one might look critically with him on that world. But Lee's structuring of the relationship between Jimmy and Girl 6 renders such a position impossible. Not only does Girl 6's work as a phone-sex operator provide financial support for Jimmy, but the film makes it clear that he is no less invested in the realm of fantasy than Girl 6 herself.

After the threat from the scary caller, Girl 6 runs to Jimmy's apartment for solace and protection. Rather than immediately showing Jimmy providing comfort, however, Lee begins the scene in his apartment with a brief montage sequence of some of Jimmy's baseball memorabilia. Jimmy is a memorabilia collector, and the buying and selling of the objects provides his only source of income. The visuals that Lee employs when Girl 6 runs to him and his discussions throughout the film evince his psychic investment in memorabilia. He hopes to make a great deal of money from the future sale of his items, but his attachment to them goes beyond any potential for profit. Baseball provides a fantasy world that Jimmy enjoys and to which he devotes almost his entire life. His criticism of phone sex comes from a position equally invested in fantasy.

The connection between the world of sports and sexuality becomes most pronounced in the film's most unusual phone-sex sequence. Girl 6 talks in a voiceover while we see a man dressed in a jockstrap, batting helmet, and cleats, as he acts out hitting a baseball. When he reaches sexual climax, he plays as if he has hit a homerun, and he bows to the fantasized applause. At this moment, the film reveals that there is no real difference between the sports fantasy and the sexual fantasy; both provide ways for the subject to organize enjoyment, and they can even overlap, as they do for this caller.

Girl 6 views fantasy as central to the subject's existence, and it endorses the investment in fantasy. When Girl 6 discovers the possibilities of fantasy through phone sex, her life undergoes a radical transformation.

She discovers a mode of enjoyment. Though *Girl 6* is in no way an endorsement of phone sex—it would be difficult to watch the film and continue to call phone-sex lines—it nonetheless reveals how the realm of fantasy offers an avenue for enjoyment that reality does not.

Though the world of phone sex functions clearly as a fantasy realm in *Girl 6,* Lee does not distinguish this realm formally from the rest of the filmic world. The editing and mise-en-scène remain relatively the same, while the difference appears dramatically within the film's content. This is Lee's common practice; most of the running time of his films occurs within the realm of fantasy. In his filmic universe, there is little space outside of this realm. Thus, though Spike Lee films often delve into the fantasies of various characters, there are few formal markers that indicate this fantasmatic turn. The case is altogether different in *She's Gotta Have It.* Here, Lee uses a formal device first enacted by Victor Fleming in *The Wizard of Oz* (1939) and used subsequently by Andrei Tarkovsky in *Stalker* (1979) and Wim Wenders in *Der Himmel über Berlin* (*Wings of Desire,* 1987), among others. Though he shoots *She's Gotta Have It* with black-and-white film stock, Lee uses color stock for one sequence. Just as in *The Wizard of Oz,* the effect is to announce to the spectator the entrance into a distinct fantasy world.

The turn to color occurs when Jamie Overstreet presents Nola Darling a birthday present in hopes of encouraging her to choose him over the other men vying for her affection. While in her apartment, Jamie covers Nola's eyes and forces her to reenact the role of Dorothy (Judy Garland) in *The Wizard of Oz.* She must repeat, "There's no place like home," and then click her heels three times. When she does so, the film cuts to a color sequence in the park. The brightness of the colors contrasts with the rest of the film, as does the scene itself, which contains two dancers performing to a musical number on an outdoor stage. The dancers enact the trajectory of a relationship in which the male offends the powerful female figure but eventually submits to her. Submission here produces a harmonious relation, which is what Jamie cannot have with Nola. The female dancer takes control of the relationship, but unlike Nola, she confines herself to one man. This scene reflects Jamie's own fantasy scenario for how their relationship would play out: he gives Nola control in exchange for a commitment to monogamy.

The use of color stock for a single
sequence in *She's Gotta Have It.*

The color sequence in *She's Gotta Have It* does not represent a
turn to fantasy in the same way as the color sequence in *The Wizard
of Oz*. Instead, this sequence is the moment at which the film depicts
a retreat from the traumatic enjoyment found in Nola's fantasy world
to the security of a more traditional fantasy—that of a stable monogamous relationship. In the color scene, despite its vibrancy, we return to
the mundane world of a traditional fantasy, in which Nola's excessive
enjoyment would no longer trouble Jamie's relationship with her. The
key to understanding the role that this scene plays in the film involves
identifying the obvious references to *The Wizard of Oz*. In Fleming's
film, the use of color signifies the turn to fantasy, but Dorothy enters this
world not of her own volition but when she is injured during a tornado.
In contrast, her return to Kansas comes about when she clicks her heels
and says, "There's no place like home."

Though Lee shoots the birthday-present scene in color, Jamie transports Nola to this fantasy world using the device that Dorothy uses to
return to Kansas in *The Wizard of Oz*. When the fantasy world becomes
too much to endure and Dorothy needs the security of home, she clicks
her heels and repeats the phrase that Glinda (Bille Burke) gives to her.

Rather than taking Dorothy into the world of color, clicking her heels and saying "There's no place like home" brings her back to the black-and-white social reality that she had earlier found so dissatisfying. Though *The Wizard of Oz* functions as the reference point for the scene in *She's Gotta Have It*, Lee plays with the allusion to highlight how Jamie's fantasy in the birthday-present scene functions as a flight from the fantasy world that he experiences with Nola. Throughout the film, Nola is a fantasmatic figure who enjoys herself beyond the bounds of social restrictions. Nola bombards Jamie with too much enjoyment, and the color sequence in the film plays out a scenario in which that enjoyment is contained. Jamie tries to bring her back to Kansas, but *She's Gotta Have It* shows that the fantasy world Nola occupies holds the key to an enjoyment that one might embrace and live out.

Fantasy is present throughout *She's Gotta Have It*, but it appears most clearly in the conclusion of *25th Hour*, a film that chronicles the last day of freedom for Monty Brogan (Edward Norton) before he must begin a seven-year prison sentence. As Monty's father James (Brian Cox) drives him to prison, he suggests the possibility of flight by driving Monty westward. As he makes this suggestion, he narrates the trajectory that Monty's future might take and uses the future tense to do so. During James's narration, we see a visual enactment of this possible future, including Monty's creation of a new identity in a small western town and his eventual reunion and marriage with his partner, Naturelle (Rosario Dawson). Lee shoots the visual depiction of this fantasy in a washed-out and faded style to differentiate it from the rest of the film, and as James finishes his narration, the film cuts back to an image of the vehicle driving along the New York highway and concludes with a close-up of Monty sleeping with his head against the car window.

25th Hour doesn't provide conclusive evidence about the course that James will take or that Monty has chosen. They may be attempting to enact the fantasy or simply continuing to the prison. But what is crucial is the role that the fantasy plays, as it appears at the end of the film. Lee includes this fantasmatic interlude to illustrate the excess that disturbs the confined world in which Monty exists. Though Monty has very limited possibilities with a long prison term looming, the very capacity for fantasy reveals how he exceeds these limitations. Even if Monty doesn't act on it, the fantasy that James concocts represents Monty's psychic freedom from the confines that the social order places on him.

Lee's embrace of fantasy involves him in a dangerous game for a filmmaker working in the shadows of Hollywood. The Hollywood system's ideological deployment of fantasy is well known and predominant. It led perhaps the greatest analyst of culture in the twentieth century, Theodor Adorno, to proclaim a sense of hopelessness about cinema as an art form. In his magnum opus *Minima Moralia*, he insists, "Every visit to the cinema leaves me, against all my vigilance, stupider and worse" (25). Adorno inveighs against the cinema because it proffers fantasies of recuperation that enable spectators to "enjoy their own dehumanization as something human, as the joy of warmth" (206). As Adorno sees it, the only attitude that one can take up relative to this joy in the cinema is a critical one; any embrace of it results in capitulation.

But the effort of Spike Lee aims at redeeming the fantasmatic possibilities of cinema in spite of the risks. Fantasy may indeed lead us to enjoy our dehumanization, as Adorno fears, but it can also mobilize an enjoyment that can vitiate the social reality in which we exist. Lee's films show a complex understanding of the political valence of fantasy. It serves to ensconce us in the stereotypes offered by our social reality, but it also exceeds this social reality by mobilizing our singular mode of exceeding it through our passion. Passion can always work for ideological purposes, but ideology never has a monopoly on passionate excesses. Lee's project as a filmmaker involves accessing our passion through an exploration of fantasy in order to free this passion from its ideological confines.

The Politics of Passion

Just as excessive passion defines character in Lee's films, it also serves as the determining factor in political questions. Characters act in the ways that they act in Lee's films on behalf of their specific form of passion. In order to show the fundamental importance of passion, Lee often marginalizes narrative. Perhaps the most famous sequence in all of Lee's films is the montage of Hollywood black stereotypes at the end of *Bamboozled*. Here, Lee indicates the presence of an excessive passion at the heart of American racism. Racism is not only oppression but also a way of structuring and directing passion.

If racist passion operates as the primary target of Lee's filmic project, next in line would be the passion that drives drug use. Everyone knows the damage that drugs do to individuals and to society as a whole, and this renders the cinematic critique of drugs almost impossible. Attempts in the cinema to expose the problems that drug use engenders often fall victim to hyperbole or didacticism. Danny Boyle's *Trainspotting* (1996) reveals the devastating effects of heroin use on Mark Renton (Ewan McGregor) and his friends. It destroys relationships and leads to criminal behavior, but Boyle doesn't shy away from making evident its attractiveness as well. Drugs provide respite from the horrors of middle-class normality, and they enable users to enjoy themselves in a way that others cannot.

In what is perhaps the great antidrug film, *Requiem for a Dream* (2000), Darren Aronofsky highlights the passion associated with drug use through a formal riff that occurs whenever the characters shoot up. A rapid juxtaposition of shots indicates their immersion in an overwhelming passion and enables the spectator to experience it as well. In the end, Aronofsky reveals the debilitating effects of drugs, most graphically when the user Harry Goldfarb (Jared Leto) must have the bottom half of his arm removed after an infection develops from the use of needles. Aronofsky further makes clear that the destructiveness of drugs has parallels within other aspects of society. Harry's mother Sara (Ellen Burstyn) has an addiction to the lottery and the television show associated with it that destroys her life as much as drugs destroy the life of her son.

In *Jungle Fever,* Lee makes the connection between the passion that accompanies drugs and other forms of passion proliferating within the rest of society even further. Drug use is an oppositional phenomenon in both *Trainspotting* and *Requiem for a Dream.* Though it is destructive for those who engage in it and for society, it is in no way constitutive of society; it exists as an alternative mode of existence. But Lee emphasizes, even more than Aronofsky, just how normal drug use—or its various social avatars—is.

When *Jungle Fever* first appeared in 1991, critics expected a return to the serious concerns of *Do the Right Thing* after the musical interlude of *Mo' Better Blues.* But they were largely disappointed. While the film received more critical appreciation than its immediate predecessor, it also fell victim to several different lines of critique. Some attacked its apparent refusal of interracial romance, while others criticized its depiction of the intense racism of lower-class Italian Americans. But the most widespread critique had its basis more in the film's form than in its content. According to this critique, *Jungle Fever* is not really a film at all but rather a series of disparate narratives edited together.

The film focuses on the interracial romance of a married black architect, Flipper (Wesley Snipes), and his Italian American assistant, Angie (Annabella Sciorra). During the depiction of the onset of this romance through its ultimate denouement in a breakup, Lee includes a multiplicity of other narrative threads. We see Flipper thrown out of the house by his wife as a result of the infidelity; Angie at odds with her family for the same reason; Angie's former boyfriend Paulie (John Turturro) struggling with the narrowness of his Italian American neighborhood; Flipper's father, the Good Reverend Doctor (Ossie Davis), ostracizing his sons for their different betrayals; and the drug world in which Flipper's brother Gator (Samuel L. Jackson) is immersed. This wide narrative range in the film makes it, at first glance, difficult to identify where the focus lies.

Even critics who displayed some affection for the film often took issue with its structure. This is the case with Benjamin Saltman, who reviewed *Jungle Fever* for *Film Quarterly*. Saltman admires Lee's ability to create a film in which "the social matrix takes precedence over intimate romance, making the sexual affair a localized sexual disaster and not a personal event" (38). In this way, Lee reverses the valence of most Hollywood depictions of romance, which use social events as the backdrop for personal development. Despite this moment of appreciation, Saltman's indictment of the film is unstinting: "It is too easy to claim that *Jungle Fever* raises significant questions; questions must be asked in coherent and significant ways. Lee's assemblage of anecdotes prevents him from entering deeply into any one of them. The very structure of the work is against analysis and for surfaces. With an entertainer's despair of depth and delight in types and observation, he gives us sketches of men and women in the context of a racist society" (40). Saltman's analysis echoes the response of many reviewers and critics, some of whom take a much more severe critical tone. For instance, Bert Cardullo asserts that "Spike Lee has yet to learn that merely to juxtapose disparate narrative strands—something that film can do almost too easily—is not to connect them, to link them with a central theme" (646). For these and other interpreters, the problem with the film stems from its lack of focus, and this lack of focus derails even the unrelenting critique of racial oppression that is the film's chief target.

By abandoning coherence, Lee does not simply dull the critical idea of the film but actually succumbs to the very societal forces that he aims to critique. The wandering style of the film imitates the undirected life of the drug user and this figure's inability to abandon an enjoyable moment for a long-term goal or, to put it in Freud's idiom, to relinquish the pleasure principle for the reality principle. Whereas the pleasure principle leads the subject to immediate gratification through the direct discharge of excitation, the reality principle uses indirection to avoid dangers and thereby brings a delayed gratification. *Jungle Fever* seems to attest to Lee's inability to adjust to the demands of thematic coherence or narrative convention, but in fact it reveals his insight into the fundamental link between drug use and the society that would condemn it.

The disparate parts of Lee's film—the conflict that the relationship between Flipper and Angie causes, the difficulties of Paulie with his father and fellow Italian Americans, and the drama of the drug addiction of Gator—all cohere around the problem of passion. Just as the intense passion for crack cocaine leads Gator to destroy his own life and damage the lives of those close to him, the promise of an unparalleled passion impels Flipper to begin an affair with Angie. In a similar way, a racist passion animates the Italian American acquaintances of Paulie and causes their hostility toward him. Passion even infects the apparent purity of the Good Reverend Doctor Purify, the father of Flipper and Gator, who lost his church because of an unnamed moral indiscretion.

When the filmic narrative jumps from one plotline to another, the spectator experiences the narrative threads, to return to Bert Cardullo's term, as "disparate." The juxtaposition seems forced and inappropriate. But Lee brings together these disparate plotlines without making an explicit connection to encourage the spectator to grasp the implicit link. Lee structures the narrative of *Jungle Fever* as a broad montage in the fashion of Sergei Eisenstein. The juxtapositions cohere not around a narrative throughline but instead center on the idea of the problem of passion. Passion doesn't simply destroy the life of the drug user. It also destroys the upright minister, the architect, and the guys hanging out at

Passion connects the disparate elements
of *Jungle Fever,* including the relationship
between Flipper and Angie.

the corner store. *Jungle Fever* asks us to see the universality of passion across the breaks in narrative logic. Passion is the force of coherence in the film.

The disparate nature of the various narrative strands emphasizes the capacity of passion to reach across race, class, and gender, and every other form of divide. Though there is no explicit relationship between a group of Italian Americans lamenting the election of David Dinkins as mayor of New York City and the massive drug use in the crack house known as the Taj Mahal, Lee's film emphasizes the significance of the connection. The phenomenon of drug use may be isolated in certain neighborhoods or certain individuals, but the appeal of drugs—the enjoyment that they promise—is ubiquitous. Lee turns from the stunning long shot of the interior of the Taj Mahal, where hundreds are smoking crack in a large darkened and smoke-filled room, to a scene in which Flipper and Angie end their relationship due to their differing forms of passion.

The connection doesn't only exist through the juxtaposition of the sequences but also through the mise-en-scène. The film moves from the darkly lit Taj Mahal to the discussion between Flipper and Angie that is shot with back lighting. The lighting creates a silhouette effect that portends the end of the relationship, but it also echoes the darkness of the Taj Mahal. Flipper and Angie cannot remain together or have feelings of genuine love for each other, according to Flipper, because of their racial difference. During this scene, Flipper and Angie sit on the bed facing away from each other to indicate the conflict. But racial difference here is just a way of formulating a difference in forms of passion. Flipper's own enjoyment is tied up in his blackness to such an extent that he cannot grasp the possibility of interracial love. Though the film doesn't make clear if this is the case for Angie or not, she does return to her neighborhood (and her father) at the end of the film, which suggests that she remains within that mode of enjoyment.

The filmic transition from the Taj Mahal to the confrontation between Flipper and Angie that ends their interracial relationship doesn't attest to Lee's failure as a filmmaker but to his overriding concern for connecting the ubiquitous passion of the crack house to the daily life of middle-class individuals who have no interest in drug use. *Jungle Fever* shows that we are all, to some extent at least, crack addicts, in the sense that we will forego everything to sustain our form of passion. Darren Aronofsky's *Requiem for a Dream* takes a step in this direction through its comparison of drug addiction with playing the lottery. But the toxic effects of excessive passion remain confined to marginalized people in Aronofsky's film. Middle-class society remains, for both Darren Aronofsky and Danny Boyle in *Trainspotting,* a zone free from the passion associated with drug use. The uniqueness of Spike Lee as a filmmaker of the drug scene lies in his refusal to separate drug users from everyone else. If forging this connection requires him to violate the demands of narrative coherence, he does so. But he does so for the sake of an unrelenting political coherence. This coherence is also present in *Clockers,* a film that brings drug use from the periphery to the center in Spike Lee's cinematic universe.

The politics of *Clockers* seems straightforward. The film condemns the racism of the predominately white police force working in a predominately black New York City neighborhood, and it equally criticizes the black drug dealers for destroying the neighborhood in another way. We see white cops joking and laughing over dead black bodies, and even the most sympathetic officer, Detective Rocco Klein (Harvey Keitel), thinks nothing of addressing a black man with the word "nigger." At the same time, the mother of a young boy who admires Strike (Mekhi Phifer), one of the dealers, tells the latter, "You are selling your own people death." Racism and the lure of drugs share responsibility for the unrelenting violence of the world that the film depicts, a world that is finally uninhabitable.

Clockers shows that the appeal of racism and drug use stems from the passion that they arouse. The only times that the white cops display any passion are when they engage in racist banter, and crack cocaine offers such an unparalleled enjoyment that it takes over the lives of those who use it. Rodney (Delroy Lindo), who controls drug traffic in the neighborhood, calls it "the world's greatest product." The film illustrates the horrors that these two forms of excessive passion produce: the impoverished and violent neighborhood is the direct result of the insistence on these forms of passion. But far from condemning passion, Lee reveals how drug dealing and use derive from the abandonment of the passion attached to the subject's singularity, and he does this through the character of Strike.

Strike's significance and position as a character is evident from the opening shot. Lee begins with a long shot of the projects with buildings symmetrical on both sides of the image. Between the buildings walks Strike alone, and he is drinking Chocolate Moo, a milk-like substance that soothes his ulcer. This opening shot indicates the extent to which Strike doesn't fit within his environment: he is alone within this world and suffers from it. This aloneness becomes more evident later when the film depicts his total alienation from his mother and even the other dealers. While they sit and talk on the benches where they deal drugs, he reads a book about trains. Strike's preoccupation with trains is his form of enjoyment that has nothing to do with his environment. Lee offers no explanation for this passion, and yet it, along with his ulcer, defines him as a character. Strike has an elaborate model train set in his apartment that he runs when he isn't working for Rodney. The train marks Strike's singular form of passion and, at the same time, his alienation from the world in which he exists. But throughout most of the film, the train serves only as a respite from this world, and in this sense, it enables him to continue to exist in an otherwise untenable situation.

As long as the train remains just a hobby for Strike, a private getaway from his public life, he remains attached to this public life that he longs to escape. Strike's singular enjoyment functions as the vehicle through which he abandons his singularity and participates in an oppressive situation. It functions as an ideological passionate attachment in the way that Judith Butler understands the term. It is a supplement to the situation and renders it tolerable. Without this supplement, Strike would act to change his world. But the point of *Clockers* is not that Strike must reject his form of passion but that he must fully embrace it. He participates in the exploitation of the neighborhood because he doesn't follow his passion for the train. He pushes his form of passion to the margin, and it is his failure in relation to his enjoyment that the film condemns.

Lee depicts the relationship between Strike's passion for the train and drug dealing through a crosscutting sequence that parallels Francis Ford Coppola's famous crosscutting between a christening and several executions at the conclusion of *The Godfather* (1972). Lee cuts between Strike running his model trains in his apartment and drug transactions going on outside. Like Coppola, Lee aims to expose the link between these two seemingly disparate phenomena. But whereas *The Godfather* makes evident the hypocrisy of Michael Corleone (Al Pacino), *Clockers* reveals the train as an alternative to drug dealing and as its supplement. The problem, however, is that Strike confines his passion for trains to models. When he prepares to leave the neighborhood and quit his life as a dealer, he crashes two model engines together. The crash of the models paves the way for Strike to enjoy a full-size train.

At the end of the film, Strike rides on a train away from New York City and away from Rodney, who now wants to kill Strike for cooperating with the police and betraying him. Strike no longer plays a part in the destruction of his neighborhood, though it is not at all clear where he will go or what he will do. Lee ends the film with Strike in the train to show him ensconced within his passion, and it is the attachment to this passion that leads Strike away from his own role in the exploitation within his neighborhood. Though *Clockers* often associates enjoyment with this exploitation, in the end it illustrates that the problem isn't too much passion but a failure to take up the singularity of one's passion.

The end of the film juxtaposes Strike riding the train away from New York with the white police officers joking over the dead body of another black man. After laughing with other cops at the murder scene, Rocco's partner, Detective Larry Mazilli (John Turturro), compares the neighborhood to "one of those self-cleaning ovens" because of the rampant self-destructive violence. Through this concluding contrast, Lee stresses the opposed ways in which passion can function politically. Strike's insistence on his singular enjoyment leads him away from drug dealing, while Mazilli's racist passion helps to sustain the neighborhood's violence by turning a blind eye to it. But Rocco, who arrives late at the scene, does not participate in the racist banter and represents an alternative.

Like Strike, Rocco, despite his use of racist epithets, doesn't fit into the typical identity associated with the other white cops. He acts to save Strike and two others in the neighborhood, Strike's brother Victor (Isaiah Washington) and Tyrone (Pee Wee Love), who commit murders that would destroy their lives. The film never makes clear why Rocco works on behalf of Victor and Tyrone, but it does show that he shares Strike's alienation from his world. After young Tyrone has shot and killed Errol (Thomas Jefferson Byrd), Rocco interrogates him. Rather than listening to Tyrone's explanation, he explains to Tyrone just what he must say in order to exculpate himself. Here, we see how Rocco's excess in relation to his environment allows him to treat the people in the neighborhood justly, in contrast to the other white police officers, who indulge in excess only in the form of their racist passion. *Clockers* thus makes clear the political implications of the relationship that one takes up to one's excess.

Lee shoots Rocco's questioning session in a highly stylized manner that removes all verisimilitude and reveals just how out of place Rocco is. As Rocco tells Tyrone what to say, he appears in a close-up in the interrogation room, but in the middle of his explanation, the film cuts to an outdoor shot that tracks along with Rocco as he moves in a circle talking to Tyrone at what seems like an increased distance. After this sequence, the film cuts to a tracking shot of Tyrone biking toward Errol and preparing to shoot him, while Rocco stands beside the bike and moves along with it. Clearly this is an impossible scene: Rocco could not stand next to a moving bike and move with it.

With the next cut, the radicality of what Rocco is doing becomes even more evident in the film's form. Lee violates the 180-degree rule and cuts to an opposed angle to show Tyrone on his bike stopped in front of Errol as Rocco says to him, "All of a sudden, there's Errol, that kid killer, standing right in front of you." After a cut to a close-up of Tyrone, the film shows Errol, and Rocco completes the story. He says, "He's got this horrible look in his beady eyes. You see him reaching." This account of the events is not factual, and Rocco knows that it is a fabrication, but he offers it to Tyrone because he doesn't want to see his life destroyed. The film never explains what differentiates Rocco from the other white cops, but it does show his refusal to participate in their forms of passion surrounding black deaths.

When Rocco drops Strike at Penn Station so that he can take the train out of New York, Strike asks Rocco why he cares, why he has saved him, his brother, and Tyrone. Rather than answer, Rocco responds by threatening to arrest Strike if he ever sees him again. One can imagine all sorts of possible responses: ethical, political, religious, or some other reasons for acting in the way that he does. But Rocco can say nothing. The critic Douglas MacFarland interprets this lack of response as an expression of disgust. He claims, "Rocco almost disgustedly tells [Strike] to get out of town and stay out. Rocco seems morally and even physically repulsed by Strike's presence. He is unable to situate Strike within his schema or good and evil" (12–13). While it is undoubtedly correct that Strike exceeds any system of good and evil, Rocco's gesture seems difficult to reconcile with contempt for Strike.

Rocco's act of bringing Strike to the train station itself transcends the framework from which he might condemn Strike, and this is what MacFarland's understanding of this scene misses. Rocco acts from a singularity akin to Strike's passion for the train, and this singularity remains irreducible to signification. *Clockers*—along with the rest of Lee's cinema—celebrates this singularity and the acts that derive from it. If passionate racism and drug use is the source of the horror of the projects, it is also the only possible solution to this horror. Rocco's singular enjoyment, like Strike's, exceeds the situation in which it exists and works to unravel that situation. This is why he can't tell Strike the reason for his actions: whatever he might say would reduce the act to the situation out of which it emerges and contextualize it.

Nowhere is the political ambivalence of enjoyment presented more straightforwardly than in *Malcolm X*. Lee divides the film into two parts, and each part illustrates a contrasting side of the politics of excessive enjoyment. In the first section, we see Malcolm Little (Denzel Washington) awash in various forms of illicit enjoyment, forms that appear to challenge the ruling social structure but actually reinforce it. Malcolm dances in the street and in a club with his friend Shorty (Spike Lee). He has sexual relationships with numerous women, including Sophia

(Kate Vernon), a white woman. He listens passionately to the radio with a group of black men as Joe Louis knocks out Billy Conn. He dresses fancily—at one point in a bright red pinstripe suit and hat. He runs numbers for a local gangster, West Indian Archie (Delroy Lindo). Finally, he organizes a group to perform robberies.

During all these activities, the film highlights Malcolm's passion. He doesn't just dress nicely but flaunts his expensive attire to arouse desire and envy. He doesn't just organize a robbery but plays Russian roulette (though he palms the bullet) with someone involved who challenges his authority. This excessive passion causes his break with West Indian Archie, a break that almost leads to Malcolm's death. As Malcolm describes himself in a voiceover, "I wasn't afraid of anything. I was an animal." Though this accurately captures Malcolm's attitude at the time, the final judgment in this statement gets it completely wrong. His lack of fear doesn't provide an index of his animality but of the excess associated with subjectivity. Where animals fight for their lives, subjects put guns to their own heads to demonstrate their fearlessness. In the first part of the film, Lee shows how this excessive passion can be channeled in socially disruptive but ultimately conformist ways. Excessive passion that manifests itself in criminality or luxury or unaccepted sexuality has the effect of securing the social structure that it appears to challenge.

Lee makes this evident through his juxtaposition of Malcolm's activities in the first part of the film with scenes from Malcolm's youth that show the Ku Klux Klan threatening his father, pillaging the family home, burning it, and finally leaving his father to die in front of an onrushing train. Though the flashback sequences serve to fill in the back story of Malcolm's youth, the manner in which the film deploys these sequences stresses the parallel between the racist passion that kills Malcolm's father and the young Malcolm's enjoyment. Of course, Malcolm is not a white bigot killing those who reject the ruling white power structure, but his passion upholds this structure in the same way rather than challenging it, as he will later in the film.

Malcolm X underlines the role that Malcolm's passion plays in sustaining his oppression by cutting from images of him enjoying himself to shots of the Klan's brutal violence against his family. On one occasion, Malcolm and Shorty are mimicking gangsters from popular films, and as Malcolm falls to the ground imitating someone having been shot, Lee uses a match cut to flashback to the murder of Malcolm's father by the Klan. The transition from the shot of Malcolm enjoying himself with Shorty to his father dying as a result of the vicious passion of the Klan connects these apparently disparate activities. Like his father, Malcolm is the victim of an excessive passion, though in Malcolm's case this excess attaches him libidinally to a social order that oppresses him. In the case of his father, the libidinal attachment is visible in the Klan's violence. They clearly enjoy their violence, which is why they perform it at night and under the cover of sheets, as if it were a sexual activity.

The association of the Klan with passion occurs visually in the film. It is not by accident that perhaps the most memorable and even sublime scene in all of Lee's cinema depicts the Klan riding away from the Little house after breaking out the windows and threatening Malcolm's father. In this scene, Lee shows four hooded Klansmen on horseback riding toward a full moon that completely encompasses them, providing a majestic backlight and creating a silhouette effect on the riders and their horses. The moon dwarfs the Klansmen, but the scene permits the spectator a touch of the sublime. The sublimity of the scene connects the spectator with the enjoyment that the Klansmen themselves experience. Though Lee obviously doesn't endorse the Klan's activity, he does make clear visually the source of its appeal, and he encourages the spectator

The visual depiction of the excess passion
of the Klan in *Malcolm X*.

to partake of this appeal as well. One must recognize the power of the excessive passion that fuels the Klan if one is to struggle against this group and what they represent. It is a different form of this excessive passion that drives Malcolm, but it is excessive passion nonetheless.

The juxtaposition of Malcolm's life with images of the violence that his family suffered at the hands of the Klan comes to an end after Malcolm's conversion to Islam and the transformation of his form of passion. The second part of the film focuses solely on Malcolm and not on white racism, even though his political activity explicitly targets this racism. Lee constructs this radical shift as a way of documenting the changed effect of Malcolm's new form of excess. Whereas Malcolm's excessive attachment of sex, drinking, gambling, and criminality functions as the perfect supplement to the brutal racism of the Klan, his political activity—a different form of excess—works to wipe out this racist excess. Through a formal change in the structure of the film, Lee shows the effect that a transformation of one's form of passion might have.

Though Malcolm's passion is clear in the first part of the film, it is less overtly evident after his conversion. In fact, he seems to have abandoned passion altogether for religious devotion, abstaining from alcohol, and monogamy. An FBI agent listening in on Malcolm's phone conversations proclaims, "Compared with King, this guy's a monk." But the second part of the film shows Malcolm's excessive commitment to racial justice and the passion that this commitment reveals. We see him preaching to cheering crowds and delivering some of his pithiest critiques of white racism, such as, "We didn't land on Plymouth Rock. Plymouth Rock landed on us." Malcolm has such passion for his political activity that he earns the enmity of the other followers of Elijah Muhammad (Al Freeman Jr.).

Malcolm X's death, as the film portrays it, is the direct result of his excessive passion. The other followers of Elijah Muhammad and Muhammad himself envy Malcolm's passion, and they attempt to destroy it. Though they do kill him, his excess lives on through those who identify with him, including the schoolchildren at the end of the film who proclaim, "I am Malcolm X." When they make this declaration, they identify not with Malcolm's social position but with how he exceeded this position—with what in Malcolm was irreducible to signification.

After Malcolm's transformation, the film encourages the spectator to engage in a similar identification. This becomes most apparent when

Malcolm makes his most forceful political act. He hears that the police have beaten Brother Johnson (Steve White). In response, Malcolm organizes members of the Nation of Islam to march to the police station where the injured Brother Johnson is being held. Outside the police station, the camera pans over a huge crowd of people chanting for justice, and in front of them stands a line of men from the Nation of Islam. Lee cuts to an interaction within the station between Malcolm and the police officer in charge, who relents and allows Malcolm to see Brother Johnson when faced with the pressure from the group outside. When Malcolm comes outside, he simply gestures, and the members of the Nation of Islam walk away, which causes the crowd to disperse. A white police officer says, "That's too much power for one man to have." This display of discipline and power indicates Malcolm's excessive relation to the police order itself. As Lee shows it, he has the power to overcome the white police force, despite the social forces backing them and despite their weapons. At this point, the film encourages the spectator to share in the passion evinced by Malcolm's ability to transcend seemingly intransigent social barriers.

Since the spectator identifies not with Malcolm's social identity but with how he exceeds this identity, critiques of the film that stress its overly masculinized portrayal of Malcolm X miss the nature of the appeal that Lee creates. Maurice E. Stevens gives voice to this lament. He notes that Lee's film "asks those seeking the promise of identification, the home of history, and the possibility of a place in the present to disavow, and in that way forget, anything but his newly racialized heteronormative image of gender (and its performance), thereby condemning African-American identity and historical agency to suffer under the weight of its own manhood, its shining black manhood" (339). The problem with this diagnosis of the film lies in its understanding of the film's deployment of identification. Rather than asking us to identify with the masculine and heterosexual figure of Malcolm X, it prompts us to identify with what exceeds this figure, an enjoyment that goes beyond his social—or masculine—identity. This is why Lee spends so much time focusing on Malcolm's excesses and so little time focusing on his identity. To identify with Malcolm X while watching the film is to disrupt the social determinants of identity itself. This identification is an identification with the excessive passion that he embodies. *Malcolm X* reveals how this passion can operate in a variety of political directions, but it insists that politics can never avoid the problem or opportunity created by excessive passion.

The role that passion plays in Spike Lee's fiction films is not surprising. Passion has been central to the cinema since its inception. From the silent era forward, numerous filmmakers have given priority to passion in their various attempts to construct a political cinema. Excessive passion predominates in the films of Sergei Eisenstein, Charlie Chaplin, and Buster Keaton, to name a few. But unlike these other filmmakers committed to marshalling passion, Lee also brings this concern to his documentary filmmaking. Of all the cinematic modes, documentary is the one that has historically avoided the question of passion more than any other. On the level of both form and content, documentaries tend to privilege informing over arousing; this marks the limitation of the documentary form as a political practice.

This limitation has become especially evident in documentaries responding to recent political events that center around passion, like the problem of the American torture of prisoners of war or enemy combatants. As Hilary Neroni makes clear, "The enjoyment present in torture . . . is not investigated in the documentaries that focus on torture and the War on Terror. The drive to reveal the unknown information seems to override any sustained exploration of the role that enjoyment plays in making torture possible in the first place" (249). This problem is not confined to documentaries focusing on torture. By attempting to privilege information over passion, the documentary as a form begins by lessening the political impact of the information that it provides. Lee attempts to counter this by bringing the commitment to excessive passion in his fiction films into his documentaries. This becomes evident in the sequel to *When the Levees Broke.*

The structure of *If God Is Willing and da Creek Don't Rise* rewrites the traditional documentary by addressing spectators in terms of their passion rather than providing them with additional knowledge. By beginning the film with the Super Bowl triumph of the New Orleans Saints, Lee emphasizes the enjoyment in the city surrounding this event. The subsequent portrayal of the continued devastation and suffering in New Orleans forms a contrast with this opening, but the contrast does not impugn the passion occasioned by the Super Bowl win. Instead, the film aims to mobilize that passion for the ends of socioeconomic justice. As *If God Is Willing* portrays it, the problem with New Orleans—and, by extension, with the rest of the country—is a lack of passion or enjoyment. Many political films throughout the history of cinema have used juxtaposition to enable spectators to connect apparently disparate phenomena, but Lee's film juxtaposes the joy of the Super Bowl win with the suffering in New Orleans to emphasize the distance between the two. The political aim of the film involves eliminating this distance, bringing the passion for the Saints into everyday New Orleans life—and thereby transforming the city and the country.

As Lee makes clear in *If God Is Willing*, passion often functions as a political problem. It leads us to focus on the New Orleans Saints rather than on the devastation in the city. But what separates Lee from most other documentary filmmakers is that the answer for him can never involve retreating from passion. We suffer from multiple forms of passion—aggression, paranoia, and so on. But at the same time, the excessive passion that we experience provides the only path to freedom. Lee creates films that criticize our excesses only to find a way to embrace them more fully.

Fight the Paranoia

Most viewers of Spike Lee films see him as first and foremost an antiracist filmmaker. This is a point that Robin R. Means Coleman and Janice D. Hamlet make in their introduction to their edited collection of essays on Lee, *Fight the Power!: The Spike Lee Reader*. They note, "Lee has consistently disseminated, through all forms of his discourses, the argument that we must become astutely conscious of the damage being done to black communities, notably, often by those external to those communities" (xx). Lee's films are only the most salient manifestation of his antiracist combat.

This is not an inaccurate impression: most of Lee's films do involve a critique of racism as it appears in all types of characters. But his critique of racism is never just a superficial moral upbraiding of those who demonstrate racist thoughts or actions. Lee's films attempt to grasp the roots of racism and to show spectators why racism is an appealing position to take up despite the obvious injustice that it involves. He locates the racist impulse in paranoia about the passionate other—the belief that someone else, someone alien, is enjoying themselves at my expense. Someone else is in the throes of passion, and this explains why I feel as if I am not. Oftentimes, of course, racism manifests itself in social institutions rather than actions or words. This type of racism would seem to be simply a question of power rather than paranoia. One group dominates another through oppressive institutions and conceives of the other group as a form of animality not worthy of equal treatment. This form of racism appears most manifestly in Lee's documentaries, such as *4 Little Girls*, *When the Levees Broke*, and *If God Is Willing and da Creek Don't Rise*. But the question remains why this racism forms and what sustains it. Institutional structures have a historical inertia that seems to operate independent of subjective acts, but in fact, they require subjects to actively prop them up at all times. And it is precisely the subject's paranoia about the other's enjoyment that sustains all our racist institutions. Even the image of the other as an animal emerges as a response to an encounter with an alien form of enjoyment that the subject cannot access and from which it retreats. To understand how racism works in all of Lee's films, one must confront the paranoia that seems almost endemic to subjectivity as such.

Paranoia attributes an excessive passion to the other. Rather than remaining within the society's strictures, the other partakes of an illicit passion by exceeding them. Paranoia sees excess everywhere except in itself, and this is exactly the logic at work in racism. Racism is itself an excess that offers an excessive passion, which is why so many people find it appealing. But at the same time, no racist views her- or himself as excessive or as enjoying the experience of racism. It is the other that experiences excessive passion, and this illicit enjoyment, according to the racist way of thinking, has prompted negative feelings about the other race.

Without paranoia about the excessively passionate other, there is no racism. All racist mythology about the other—ideas of sexual promiscuity, drunkenness, body odor, laziness, and so on—has its origin in the belief that the racial other enjoys in a fashion that the subject itself cannot and that this excessive passion threatens the subject's own possibilities for enjoying itself. This understanding of how racism works appears in many of Spike Lee's films. But ironically, it is in *Summer of Sam*, one of Lee's films with almost no focus at all on black characters, where the critique of racism through an analysis of paranoia is most pronounced. The role that *Summer of Sam* plays in Lee's analysis of the logic of racism becomes evident in the various relationships that the film sets up—between Ritchie (Adrien Brody) and the Dead End Gang, between Vinny (John Leguizamo) and his wife Dionna (Mira Sorvino), and between the serial killer David Berkowitz (Michael Badalucco) and his victims, among others. The central position that the logic of racism occupies in the film leads the critic Dan Flory to call it "a subtle form of racial analysis" that works to "thematize these suspicions of difference and transform this Bronx tale into a parable about racial lynching" (262). In *Summer of Sam*, as Flory correctly points out, we see a lynching party come for a white character who inhabits the position of the ostracized and enjoying other, a position typically inhabited by black subjects in American society. But Lee goes further than just displaying a modern-day lynching; he probes the psychic determinants that produce such horrors. There is no lynch mob without paranoia about the passionate other.

As Lee's films show, people become paranoid because they imagine that others access a passion that they cannot. The characters see excess everywhere around them except in themselves. This is true of almost every character in *Summer of Sam.* The film depicts the effect of the Son of Sam killings on the city of New York, and it illustrates that these killings occasion an outbreak of paranoia, following from the belief that the serial killer has stolen the community's passion. Ritchie, who displays his own idiosyncratic passion through his punk attire and hairstyle, becomes the target of vigilante justice, which views him as a thief of passion. This same structure is at work in many of Lee's films and constitutes the contribution to an understanding of how racism works.

In *Summer of Sam,* no one is immune to excessive passion. Even Dionna, an apparently innocent victim of her husband Vinny's philandering and drug addiction, exhibits an excessive devotion to her father and to religion that the film highlights. Excess is ubiquitous. R. Barton Palmer claims, "Breakdowns in sanity, emotional restraint, humaneness, and respect for the social order are revealed not as deviations but as symptomatic, even exemplary" (64). Mikal J. Gaines adds, "Nearly all the film's characters exhibit excessive and decadent behavior" (151). The excesses proliferate throughout the film because excess provides the possibility for enjoyment, but at the same time, it confronts others with an image of passion that creates a sense that their own passion is at risk or has been stolen.

The film opens with an attempt to explain what drove David Berkowitz to kill, and this will provide the matrix for almost all the subsequent actions of the film's other characters as well. After the reporter Jimmy Breslin introduces the film by discussing changes in New York City since the summer of 1977 (when the film is set), Lee begins with a shot tracking across Berkowitz's apartment. A dog barks incessantly on the audio track, and we see Berkowitz lying face down on his bed screaming repeatedly, "Shut that dog up." Here, it is the passion of the dog and its owner, embodied by the nonstop barking, that disrupts his own ability to enjoy. The dog that barks nonstop signifies enjoyment not because the dog itself enjoys barking but because it indicates the owner's lack of concern for others and for the social order as such. The private passion that the owner derives from the dog has more value than the imposition on the owner's neighbors. In this sense, the barking dog functions like loud music, public screaming, or blowing smoke in someone's face. In the film, the barking dog stands in for all the passion that confronts Berkowitz—passion that others seem to experience and that he can only observe. He seeks relief from this oppressive passion as it manifests itself in the attractive women and sexually engaged couples that he targets with violence. As Lee shows, there is no difference between the confrontation with the barking dog outside his apartment and that of the couple displaying their sexual attraction for each other in a car, a semipublic space.

Summer of Sam makes this point clearly through the cut that occurs just after the scene in Berkowitz's apartment. Over a black screen, the song "Fernando" from the pop group ABBA begins to play. The upbeat melody creates a contrasting mood with the opening scene, but the lyrics nostalgically discussing the exploits of former freedom fighters suggest a unique moment of excessive passion that the singer shared with Fernando, the song's addressee. This unique moment is precisely what Berkowitz feels that the world has deprived him of, and his killing in the next scene follows from this sense of having been cheated. The film shows two women talking together in a car while the song plays on with a dog barking in the background. The barking dog establishes continuity with the earlier scene and aligns the two women with the dog. Just as Berkowitz cannot find any relief from the noise of the dog, neither is there any respite for him from the sexuality of the women. The following scene evokes the ubiquity of excessive passion in another form.

Vinny drives with Dionna to a dance club, where they dance in a shot that creates the impression that they are alone despite the crowd in the club. The music and mise-en-scène here enhance the sense of passion present in the earlier scenes. Vinny and Dionna are well dressed in the style of the late 1970s, and a line outside the club indicates its popularity. When they dance, the film creates the idea that their enjoyment transports them from the confines of their world when everyone else disappears from the image.

After the dance, Vinny offers to drive Dionna's cousin home from the club and then return for Dionna. While doing so, he has sex with her in his car, and Berkowitz watches. Though Berkowitz ends up shooting another couple, it is clear that he targets Vinny's illicit passion and that he almost shoots Vinny. When Berkowitz shoots the other couple, the audio track again includes a dog's bark, which highlights the connection between the dog and sexuality, both of which confront Berkowitz with the theft of his passion. Though Berkowitz is not the primary focus of *Summer of Sam,* he is an exemplary character because he sees excess all around him, and yet he himself is the real figure of excess.

For the rest of the characters in the film, Berkowitz represents the primary threat to their passion. If they have sex in the back of a car or even leave their homes at night, they must worry that he'll kill them. But Berkowitz himself kills out of the belief that his own passion has been stolen. Lee establishes this dynamic between Berkowitz and the other characters to show how the idea of stolen passion informs how everyone enjoys—even the primary thief of passion himself. Though one can certainly see the Dead End Gang's attack of Ritchie as a paradigmatic form of lynch-mob violence, Berkowitz's shootings also follow the same form. Though he is an individual, Berkowitz acts from the motivations that drive the Dead End Gang to assault Ritchie, whom they believe to be the Son of Sam.

The Dead End Gang—composed of leader Joey T. (Michael Rispoli), Anthony (Al Palagonia), and Brian (Ken Garito), with peripheral members Woodstock (Saverio Guerra) and Bobby Del Fiore (Brian Tarantina)—are figures of obscene passion. We never see them working except when dealing drugs, and their drug use and indulgence in violent outbursts reveal their refusal to respect social restrictions. Though they see themselves as policing outcasts and criminals, they themselves are the real danger to their neighborhood. In this sense, they follow the same paranoid logic as Berkowitz: they feel themselves threatened by the passionate other while all along perpetuating a passion that itself is far more dangerous than what they fear in the other.

The absolute horror of the passionate other becomes most fully evident when Joey T. and Anthony enter the punk club CBGB that Ritchie frequents. Lee depicts them walking through the densely packed club in slow motion, as Joey holds a handkerchief over his mouth as if to protect himself from the toxicity of the atmosphere inside, and Anthony holds his hands over his ears to keep out the threatening music. A brief montage sequence of singing and dancing combines with the loud music to embody the passion that overwhelms the two members of the Dead End Gang in CBGB. After they leave, Anthony tells Joey, "I could take ten showers. I'd still feel fucking dirty." Then, Joey beats up a youth dressed in punk attire who proclaims that the Red Sox are his favorite baseball team. Anthony's exclamation and Joey's violence are responses to the bombardment of foreign passion that they experience in the punk

Ritchie's enjoyment in *Summer of Sam*. |

club. The trauma of excessive passion and the attempt to destroy it recurs throughout *Summer of Sam*, but two points in the film stand out for their depictions of this excess.

The most famous sequences of the film are the two montage sequences that Lee constructs using songs from the Who. The first, in the middle of the film, involves Ritchie playing the Who's "Baba O'Reilly" on his turntable while singing and playing guitar along with the music. After Ritchie begins the song, the montage begins with Berkowitz killing someone in a car before it cuts back to Ritchie as he continues to play guitar and then as he appears in a gay strip club. Subsequent shots depict Ritchie cutting up a stuffed doll on the stage, Ritchie buying the new guitar that he is playing, someone shooting up with heroin, fans cheering Reggie Jackson at Yankee Stadium, the Dead End Gang beating someone, the guitar falling to the ground, and Ritchie dancing with Ruby. The montage concludes with a close-up of Berkowitz's mouth as the song ends. The series of images, combined with the oft-repeated refrain of the song, "teenage wasteland," indicates the unleashing of passion throughout the filmic world. There is nowhere in Lee's New York City that one can escape the image of proliferating passion.

The second montage sequence employing the Who's music occurs at the end of the film. The song "Won't Get Fooled Again" plays as the Dead End Gang and Vinny come to beat up Ritchie and reveal him as the Son of Sam to the neighborhood mafia leader Luigi (Ben Gazzara). Lee juxtaposes their assault on Ritchie with the police bringing Berkowitz to headquarters amid a mob of people screaming for his punishment. Though Ritchie is an innocent victim in this situation, the montage has the effect of paralleling him with Berkowitz, who is clearly guilty. For Lee, the guilt or innocence of the figures in these scenes is immaterial. What matters is the role they play within the paranoid structure of the collective psyche that assembles to confront them.

As the film cuts back and forth between the two events, the words of the reporter at the police headquarters, John Jeffries (Spike Lee), overlap the contrasting visuals. As he describes the rage of the crowd watching Berkowitz brought in, his words apply equally to the Dead End Gang as they assault Ritchie. Berkowitz and Ritchie function as figures of sacrifice in this montage: the mobs view them as threats to their own passion, but they themselves enjoy their aggression toward these embodiments of passion. This final montage makes clear how paranoia produces passion through the assault on it.

Lee's choice of music is even more apropos than in the first montage sequence. The title of the song, "Won't Get Fooled Again," bespeaks the logic of paranoia in the most direct fashion. The paranoid subject sees her- or himself as the constant dupe and is determined to do what it takes to avoid remaining in this position. Rather than allow the other to continue to enjoy at their expense, paranoid subjects attempt to destroy the other's capacity for passion and to recuperate their own lost enjoyment. They act so that they won't get fooled again, but this effort always fails because passion exists only through loss.

The follow-up film to *Summer of Sam*, *Bamboozled*, also confronts the problem of paranoia concerning the other's passion, but in this film the relationship between paranoia and racism becomes fully evident. The film recounts the creation by Pierre Delacroix (Damon Wayans) of a satirical television program in the form of a minstrel show. Delacroix hopes to use the program to induce the firing of himself and his boss, Thomas Dunwitty (Michael Rapaport), but it becomes a huge popular success, unleashing previously unacceptable racist tropes, including the use of blackface over Delacroix's objections. The show, entitled *Mantan: The New Millennium Minstrel Show,* takes place on a plantation and features two street performers, Manray (Savion Glover) and Womack (Tommy Davidson), wearing blackface in the roles of Mantan and Sleep 'n Eat. The popularity of the show stems from the paranoia that it uncovers: while watching the show, spectators believe that they access the black passion that existed on the plantation.

Dunwitty, the white network executive, exemplifies this attitude. The décor of his office (posters of famous black athletes like Mike Tyson, African art, and so on) and his way of speaking (the use of the word "nigger") indicate his investment in the idea of black enjoyment. The film also reveals that he has a black wife, which underlines this investment. Once the show becomes popular, Dunwitty becomes a great fan, going so far as to don blackface like the characters in the show. Even though Dunwitty doesn't kill anyone like David Berkowitz or beat the other like the Dead End Gang, his paranoia is perhaps just as destructive. As a network executive heading the production of *Mantan,* he disseminates and validates the image of a hidden black passion to millions of viewers.

The problem isn't that Dunwitty and other white fans of *Mantan* aren't authentic in their commitment to blackness. This is the critique authored by Beretta Smith-Shomade, who claims that "underneath it all Dunwitty's whiteness (and thus his privilege) remains; his black wipes off" (236). Certainly, Dunwitty isn't authentically black, but the real damage that he does comes from his belief in black authenticity and his effort to access it. One dons blackface only when one believes in black authenticity, even though blackface is clearly an inauthentic mask. The mask—like the racist trinkets that Delacroix collects—promises to put the wearer in touch with an authenticity that he or she necessarily cannot fully inhabit.

Paranoia about black passion requires an idea of black authenticity, but it also demands that this authenticity remain visible but also forever just out of reach. This allows those invested in paranoia to sustain their paranoia. If they ever were really to access blackness, they would recognize that the passion they attributed to it does not exist—that where they imagine passion, there is nothing but the travails that everyone suffers and the additional suffering that comes from occupying an oppressed identity. There is no such thing as authentic blackness, but the sham blackness of blackface, as *Bamboozled* shows, works to keep alive the idea of it. Appearances deceive by creating the impression that the authentic resides hidden beneath them, when they in fact cover an absence.

When the show premieres, Lee cuts from the racist depictions in the show to audience reactions to reveal the real passion that the show produces. But this passion depends on the belief that the minstrel show touches on authentic black passion. The way that Lee shoots the audience reaction makes this clear. We initially see shots of disturbed and even shocked audience members. But when white audience members see their black counterparts begin to laugh, they laugh as well. The whites wait for the black laughter to validate what they are seeing and to provide reassurance that the racism present in the minstrel show does arouse black passion.

Disgusted by what Pierre has unleashed, his assistant Sloan (Jada Pinkett Smith) shoots him at the end of the film, and as he dies, she plays a video montage of racist imagery from the history of Hollywood on the television in his office. These are the last images that Pierre sees, and they punctuate his life. In addition, this montage sequence is one of the high points of Spike Lee's cinematic career. He not only manages to bring together a series of racist images that indict Hollywood across the board, but he also shows precisely how blackness functions as an indicator of the ultimate enjoyment. At the same time, the film highlights the absence of enjoyment at the precise point where it seems to be most evidently present.

The montage includes the famous Gus chase scene from D. W. Griffith's *The Birth of a Nation*, in which a black man (a white actor in blackface) reveals himself as a sexual predator threatening southern white femininity, as well as numerous images of black characters performing obsequious and stereotypical acts for white audiences within the image and without. The black characters in the montage sequence all appear to be enjoying themselves if we consider each image independently. Lee constructs the montage, however, to make this approach impossible. Like Sergei Eisenstein's celebrated montage sequence depicting the slaughter of civilians on the Odessa Steps in *Battleship Potemkin* (1925), Lee's montage of Hollywood racism forces us to see from the perspective of the victims rather than from that of the oppressors who look on and see untrammeled passion.

Lee turns to montage to counter the paranoid response to the image of black passion. *Bamboozled* demands that we look differently to avoid seeing the passion that is present and to recognize the trauma that isn't. When the montage sequence brings the numerous scenes of black passion together, we can grasp that the image of enjoyment obscures the trauma of black subjectivity in America. But seeing this requires seeing what isn't there, what exists only in the cuts that join the images together and not in the images themselves. The ability to see absence, the capacity for recognizing trauma amid the image of passion, is the only antidote for paranoia about the passionate other, and this is the antidote that *Bamboozled* proposes.

Lee indicates this absence formally at other points in the film as well, though the montage sequence represents the high point. When Pierre Delacroix organizes a meeting for the writers of the minstrel show, the structure of the scene makes clear Delacroix's own absence within the white world of the network. Delacroix points out the absence of any black writers for the show, but the white writers around the table refuse to countenance this absence and acknowledge the institutional racism that produced it. One of the writers claims, "I think it would be good to have some . . . African-American writers, but for whatever reason, they're not here." The writer recognizes the absence but can't bring himself to recognize the structure behind the absence.

But at least the first writer does confront the fact of this absence to some extent. Another writer at the meeting proclaims that his experience of black characters on television in the 1970s authorizes him to write for the show. He says, "My first experience of the black people . . . of Africa . . . is that . . . these shows like *The Jeffersons*." This leads other writers to point out black television shows that impacted them, and while they do so, Lee cuts to short clips from these shows, all of which depict images of black passion.

While the white writers at this meeting fail to recognize the absence of blackness, Lee works to make it apparent to the spectator. The scene begins with a long shot of the conference table with Pierre at the head of the table. The scene concludes with an identical shot from an exact reverse angle, a shot from Pierre's perspective, which reveals an empty chair in the position that Pierre occupied in the initial shot. Lee frames the scene with the shot and reverse shot to signal the absence of blackness within the white world of the television network, even when it comes to writing for a black show.

By forcing us to see Pierre's absence in the writers' meeting despite the fact that he runs the meeting, Lee suggests a new mode of seeing that takes absence rather than presence as its point of departure. When we look for what is present, we see images of the passionate other, and this leads to paranoia about the threat to our own passion. But when we see absence and trauma in the seemingly complete image of the passionate other, paranoia loses its hold on us. No one who recognizes absence—no one who sees the cut in the cinema—can succumb to paranoia's appeal.

One of Lee's aims in making a documentary about Hurricane Katrina was to expose the paranoia that developed around this natural disaster and transformed it into a political catastrophe. *When the Levees Broke* chronicles the anxiety about unrestrained black passion that Katrina unleashed. Even though the black population disproportionately suffered from the storm's devastation, paranoia about out-of-control black passion proliferated in the hurricane's aftermath. Lee's interviews demonstrate how a series of myths of rampant criminality—looting, murdering, and even raping babies in the Superdome—developed among local authorities and in the national media. In one case, it is the black police chief who is responsible for the dissemination of the most horrific paranoid speculation.

Though the film does point out instances of actual black looting, the overwhelming tragedy of Katrina results from political indifference and the white upper- and middle-class paranoia about the threat of black theft and violence. Paranoid whites shoot black men walking down the street, and armed local police officers prevent largely black crowds from walking from downtown New Orleans to safety in a largely white community over a bridge. In each case, paranoia about black passion—and its inherent violence directed at whites—becomes the source of violence. It is also the source of the institutional indifference to black suffering. Paranoia enables subjects to perceive themselves as responding to a threat while they are actually the embodiment of the threat. The danger resides in those who are paranoid, not those whom the paranoid suspect.

Lee's filmic efforts to fight against paranoia extend into the most socially fraught territory not in his depictions of rampant racism in *Bamboozled* but with his turn to clerical child molestation in *Red Hook Summer*. The child molester is one of the chief sites for paranoid speculation today. Though child molestation is without question a traumatic horror for the child victim, the societal view of the molester as the worst form of deviant suggests that we attribute to the child molester an excessive enjoyment that occurs at the expense of innocent children. By creating sympathy for the child molester before exposing him as a molester, Lee attempts to undermine this paranoia, to reveal that the molester lives a tortured life and not a life replete with obscene enjoyment.

Red Hook Summer returns to the Brooklyn setting of earlier Lee films and focuses on a young boy from Atlanta, Flik (Jules Brown), whose mother brings him to spend the summer with his father Enoch (Clarke Peters), a minister in the Red Hook neighborhood. The film shows a tumultuous relationship between the highly religious Enoch and the secular Flik, but it also presents each character in a relatively positive light. Though Enoch's religious displays are excessive and he places strict demands on Flik, Enoch does seem to care for him like a loving grandfather. At one point, he even takes Flik kayaking for the first time in his life, and Flik clearly enjoys this experience that he otherwise might never have had.

But roughly three quarters of the way through the film, the spectator's relationship to Enoch undergoes a complete transformation. A young man, Blessing Rowe (Colman Domingo), comes to his small church and accuses Enoch of molesting him years earlier when he was a minister in Georgia. Lee uses his signature dolly shot to show Rowe moving toward Enoch. Rowe claims, "You molested me. I was just a boy." Though Enoch at first denies the accusation, he later admits to it, and the film reveals the molestation scene in a flashback framed by scenes of Enoch confessing. After the news of Enoch's past becomes public, a local drug dealer and would-be rapper beats Enoch severely with the church tambourine.

The positive account of Enoch before the revelation and the depiction of the brutal beating after it have the effect of rendering him less monstrous. Though Lee does not defend the actions of the clerical child molester or even necessarily want to create sympathy for him, he does attempt to deflate the power that this image has over our collective imagination and to militate against the paranoia concerning this figure. Enoch is not a character replete with obscene enjoyment but a damaged man who has no attachments in his life. Through the character of Blessing Rowe, the film illustrates the damage that child molestation does. But our struggle against it cannot devolve into paranoia about the molester because, in doing so, it ceases to be concerned for the child and begins to function as a source of social cohesion through paranoia—and paranoia is always, for Lee, an oppressive psychic structure.

Paranoia is the driving force behind various forms of oppression, inclusive of racism. We attribute to the other a unique capacity for enjoyment that threatens or destroys our own, and we seek to contain or eliminate this threat. But the paranoid subject fails to recognize that the experience of a threatened or lost enjoyment is not the result of the malfeasance of the other. This loss inheres within every form of passion. When we experience passion, our passion occurs through the other or outside ourselves. We enjoy what we have lost. This is why paranoia necessarily blinds us to the traumatic structure of our subjectivity. As Slavoj Žižek puts it in *Tarrying with the Negative*, "What we conceal by imputing to the Other the theft of enjoyment is the traumatic fact that

we never possessed what was allegedly stolen from us" (203). Through
their unrelenting critique of paranoia, Lee's films, especially *Summer
of Sam,* enable us to gain insight into the nature of how we enjoy, to
embrace the passion of the other as our own. It is only in this way that
we can struggle against the tendency to racism that inheres within the
excesses of subjectivity itself.

The Costs of Community

Through the exclusion that it authorizes, paranoia helps to constitute
a sense of community, and this is why Lee takes up a skeptical attitude
toward our traditional conceptions of community. Community is possible for Lee, but it requires a rethinking that avoids any constitutive
exclusion. His films indicate the role of excess in constituted community. Communities, as they are typically produced, do not form through
shared interests or a common aim. There is no positive feature of society
in common that has the power to create and sustain a community because this positive feature cannot engender the passionate attachment
necessary for investment in the community. Communities require an
act through which members invest themselves in the communal bond,
and this occurs through an excessive attachment to a common idea or
object. As a result, communities necessarily involve violent exclusion.

In order to take up an excessive attachment to the source of the
communal identity, this source of identity must appear particular and
not universal. That is, it must enable the community members to distinguish themselves from everyone else. This is why community demands
exclusion. Without exclusion, the excessive dimension of the community,
the attachment to the community's idea or object, loses its appeal. Lee
makes clear that a community organizes its enjoyment through the act of
exclusion itself, which has the effect of calling into question the very idea
of community. Every community has this violent underside of exclusion,
but most often it remains hidden. One of Lee's projects as a filmmaker
involves exposing and critiquing it. This project runs throughout Lee's
films, though it is most pronounced in *Crooklyn* and *Jungle Fever.*

Crooklyn is Lee's film most devoted to the idea of community. It takes
place largely within the Bedford-Stuyvesant neighborhood of Brooklyn in
1973, and it depicts a place where people seem genuinely engaged with

and concerned about each other. The beginning of the film establishes the sense of community that recurs throughout, and it does so by focusing on the various games that children and adults play. In the opening credit sequence, we see boys racing against each other, girls jumping rope, and adults playing games as well. This opening sequence places enjoyment at the heart of the community, but the enjoyment also depends on an act of exclusion, which is the fundamental problem, as Lee sees it, with all forms of community.

In the United States, of course, community often forms around the exclusion of blackness. The community continues to rely on this excluded part, but those who are black must embody the outside for the community to constitute itself. The fact that blackness occupies this position is not at all necessary; any identity can play the part of the excluded for the sake of the community. What is essential is the logic of community that leads to the exclusion, not its particular content. To lay bare this logic apart from its typically black content, Lee depicts a white man playing the role of the excluded other in *Crooklyn,* a film where the community itself is primarily black.

The excluded white man is Tony Eyes (David Patrick Kelly), a neighbor of the Carmichael family, which is the focus of the film. Though *Crooklyn* reveals Tony Eyes behaving antisocially and at times disturbing the peace of the neighborhood, he nonetheless fulfills a structural role that enables the community to congeal around him. The film introduces the spectator to Tony Eyes early on, when his loud music disrupts a Carmichael dinner. Here Lee reverses a common stereotype that associates loud music with black rather than white subjects, a stereotype that Lee himself employs with the character of Radio Raheem in *Do the Right Thing.* When the loud music begins to blare during the dinner, the father, Woody (Delroy Lindo), goes to the window and screams at Tony to turn it down. But loud music is not is the only reason for his ostracism. Tony Eyes also has a dirty and smelly apartment that occasions the neighborhood's disdain, and whenever the neighbors attack him, they inevitably reference this smell.

But the offensive qualities of Tony Eyes do not mitigate his position in the film for the other characters and for the community. It is a community that forms around mocking and excluding Tony Eyes, and those who belong to this community, including the entire Carmichael family, revile him for his excessive enjoyment, precisely what whites throughout American history linked to an excluded blackness. Tony plays his music too loud, fails to clean up properly after himself and his dogs, and appears to indulge in perverse sexuality, which is hinted at when Woody labels him a "faggot." Tony's excess provides an occasion for the community to disavow its own excess through his exclusion.

But at the same time, the film makes it clear that the community requires Tony's excessiveness in order to exist at all. Members of the community otherwise at odds with each other come together in their shared revulsion at the figure of Tony Eyes. Tommy La La (Jose Zuniga) bonds with the Carmichael children when he breaks a bottle on Tony's door and accompanies this gesture with a series of homophobic slanders. The bond that Tony produces is especially evident just after the Carmichael mother, Carolyn (Alfre Woodard), takes Nate (Chris Knowings) to task for failing to eat his black-eyed peas. While Nate struggles with his peas, Woody brings ice cream for the children, which adds to the tension between Carolyn, who is trying to enforce some discipline, and Woody and the children, who want to enjoy themselves beyond the constraints that she sets up. Nate finally eats some peas but then throws them up. Just after this depiction of the opposition between Carolyn and her children, Lee cuts to a shot of Carolyn's son Wendell (Sharif Rashed) strewing the Carmichael trash on the property of Tony Eyes.

When Tony catches Wendell in the midst of this act, he reprimands him and begins a quarrel. Even though we see Carolyn at odds with her children just prior to this incident, she immediately intervenes on Wendell's behalf against Tony, as do other members of the community. Of course, a mother will almost always defend her child against a neighbor, but the vehemence with which Carolyn criticizes Tony and takes the side of her son suggests that Tony's exclusion here facilitates the parental and the communal bond.

Lee shoots the argument that ensues between Carolyn and Tony in an unexpected way: rather than show it in a standard shot/reverse shot sequence focusing on the face of the character speaking, Lee cuts between side angle shots of the two. As a result of this formal choice, it is as if Carolyn and Tony are not even speaking to each other, even though we know that they are. The sequence highlights their spatial and psychic separation, a separation that leaves Tony on the outside of the community. The argument is resolved when Vic (Isaiah Washington), a tenant of the Carmichaels, returns home and punches Tony in the face. This final act in the sequence makes evident the breadth of the bond that exists through Tony's ostracism. When Vic punches Tony, he earns the accolades of everyone else in the neighborhood, though the police eventually come and arrest him.

Though the costs of community become clear in *Crooklyn*, the film does not take an entirely critical view. The celebratory opening credit sequence highlights the enjoyment that the Brooklyn neighborhood provides, and the complete absence of enjoyment that Troy experiences when she leaves the neighborhood to stay with her relatives buttresses a positive assessment of the community in Brooklyn. Nonetheless, Lee never provides a wholehearted embrace of this community. The depiction of the necessary exclusion and the account of various antagonisms within the community (and the Carmichael family) reveal the underside that every community represses. *Crooklyn* stresses the persistence of this underside, but in the earlier *Jungle Fever,* the underside makes its presence felt at almost every moment of the film.

Nowhere in Lee's cinema do the costs of community become more pronounced than in *Jungle Fever,* a film that recounts the extramarital and interracial romance between Flipper and Angie. Flipper is a racially conscious and conscientious black man, and Angie is an Italian American woman who displays some fascination with blackness but otherwise professes (and generally demonstrates) the belief that race should not constitute a societal barrier. After a unique and significant credit sequence, *Jungle Fever* begins with an establishing shot of a Harlem neighborhood, where a paperboy is delivering papers. This shot establishes the community in which much of the film will take place. We then see a close-up of the newspaper as it is thrown through the air and lands on a building stoop. The camera cranes up from the paper and enters (in an homage to the opening of Hitchcock's *Psycho* [1960]) through an open window to a scene in the bedroom of a couple having sex.

This scene of the married couple, Flipper and his spouse Drew (Lonette McKee), having sex while their young daughter, Ming (Veronica Timbers), listens to the sounds and smiles in her bedroom, combined with the opening shot of the peaceful neighborhood, creates a sense of harmony. But the film establishes this sense of harmony only to reveal how it depends on violent acts of exclusion that eventually will reveal the illusory status of the harmony itself. The affair between Flipper and Angie disrupts the seemingly perfect marriage, and it brings to the surface the community's dependence on exclusion to sustain the facade of harmony. Though we never see a similar facade in the Italian neighborhood, the exclusion works even more so there. The affair results in Flipper being thrown out of his house, but Angie receives a beating from her father and verbal abuse from her brothers in addition to the ostracism.

At first, Flipper appears to be someone committed to his identity as a black man, and the film seems to endorse Flipper's position. He asks the architectural firm where he works to hire an African American assistant, and when the two owners hire Angie instead, he protests. Their rebuttals about colorblindness echo hackneyed defenses against affirmative-action policies, and Lee depicts the confrontation between Flipper and them using a series of 360-degree tracking shots that formally emphasize how their ideas fall within the narrow confines of a racist social situation.

Later, the film's most celebrated scene shows a war council of black women who come to succor Drew after Flipper's infidelity. During this free-flowing discussion, the women lament the reluctance of black men to date black women and the attempts by white women to seduce these men. Though there are dissenting voices who themselves date white men, the prevailing attitude of the war council is one of racial solidarity and a lament over its betrayal. Though the film doesn't offer an explicit endorsement of this view, it does present the idea in an appealing scene.

But what most supports a reading of the film that focuses on racial solidarity and even purity is the denouement of the relationship between Flipper and Angie. They break up because their bond appears rooted not in genuine attraction but in curiosity about the racial other. On their last night together, Flipper argues this point straightforwardly. He claims that he was interested in Angie simply because she is white and that race was also the sole reason for her interest in him. Hence, love could not arise out of this conjunction.

The failure of Flipper's relationship with Angie provides support for identifying his statements to her with the film itself, and this is the position that certain critics take up. Erica Chito Childs argues that the film "presents interracial relationships as a betrayal of the black community" (110). Others go even further. In her analysis of interracial representations in *Jungle Fever*, Diana R. Paulin criticizes the film for its espousal of racial purity (despite its flirtation with challenging this idea). She notes, "*Jungle Fever* effectively reinscribes the notion that interracial love is the result of irrational, racialized, heated passion—which manifests itself as a sickness—confirming the dominant belief, that interracial sexual relations are wrong or immoral. By naming this intimate black/white desire a 'fever,' the film serves to reproduce the notion that interracial desire is transgressive and that it contaminates pure blood lines" (168). Paulin's interpretation of the film depends on taking what particular characters say—including Flipper and his friend Cyrus (Spike Lee)—at face value, even as we see the film discredit them in unambiguous terms.

When Flipper tells Cyrus about his affair, Cyrus gives it the titular label "jungle fever," a label that also functions as an ethical indictment. As Paulin suggests, to call interracial sex "jungle fever" is to suggest that it is illicit, unethical, and motivated purely by the idea of transgression. Even though Spike Lee himself plays Cyrus, it is clear that he is not the voice of the film in this instance and that the film calls the term "jungle fever" into question at the same time that it employs it. The mere presence of Lee appearing in one of his films almost always serves as a warning sign that this character is not to be trusted; Lee uses himself as an actor in this way as a counterpoint to his direction. Though Flipper swears Cyrus to secrecy about the affair, Cyrus immediately betrays his friend's confidence and tells his wife, Drew's best friend, which has the effect of destroying Flipper's family life. Just as Flipper cannot trust Cyrus to keep his secret, the spectator cannot trust Cyrus's analysis of Flipper's relationship.

Likewise, Flipper's own condemnation of the relationship as simply a case of interracial curiosity fails to resonate because of his own status when articulating this analysis. The devastated look on Angie's face when Flipper claims that she is incapable of love for him reveals that, for her at least, this has not been a case of mere curiosity. In order to love Flipper, she had to endure ostracism from her community and physical abuse from her father. Interracial curiosity alone could not sustain her through this ordeal, and this makes Flipper's indictment of Angie seem preposterous. This conversation is one of the points at which, as Celia R. Daileader maintains, the film "criticizes black bigotry, and exposes the fault-lines within the black community introduced by questions of racial pedigree, authenticity, and class" (210). The final conversation between Flipper and Angie concludes with Angie having the last word, and what she says identifies Flipper's view of their relationship with that of her family. Though the film does not characterize Flipper as a racist like Angie's family, it does highlight his inability to see the incompleteness of black identity itself and thus the possibility of love between black and white.

Jungle Fever cannot be an argument for racial purity or against interracial romance because it reveals the exclusion that every racial or ethnic community depends on. The attempts to guard racial purity occur either on behalf of a racist ideology (as in the case of Angie's family and others in the Italian neighborhood) or in response to it (as in the case of the war council), but both forms, though not presented as equally abhorrent, make the same error. They begin with the premise of self-identical wholeness, and they fail to see that this wholeness doesn't just demand exclusion but emerges out of exclusion. A bond develops among the Italian Americans through their shared revulsion at the idea of interracial romance, and a bond also develops among the disparate black woman around the image of white women trying to steal black men. The film exposes the constitutive role of this excluded excess.

Though *Jungle Fever* ends where it begins (with Flipper and Drew having sex in their bedroom while their daughter Ming listens and smiles), the conclusion does not imply a synthesis that overcomes the disruption that has occurred during the narrative. Flipper returns to his family after Angie leaves him, but he remains a guest in the house and has not yet moved back in, though the signs point in this direction. His continued status as an exile at the end of the film is nonetheless significant. Lee refuses to show the restoration of the community but instead arrests the filmic narrative on the image of Flipper exiled and walking alone down a Harlem street. Here, he insists on highlighting what doesn't fit within the community and what the community cannot smoothly reintegrate.

In the film's final image, a female crack addict approaches Flipper and offers to perform oral sex on him—"I'll suck your big, black dick," she says—for two dollars. Horrified, Flipper screams, "No!" And then the film ends. Not only do we see Flipper left in a position of exile, but the film also confronts us with another figure of excess who disrupts the potential for community. The crack addict who prostitutes herself for drugs is another barrier to the formation of a stable black community in the Harlem neighborhood. Her excessive enjoyment of crack leads her to destroy her life, and it also renders community impossible. Addiction leads to crime, violence, and prostituting oneself, all of which militate against stable social relations.

But despite this concluding image, *Jungle Fever* does present the communal bond as a possibility. For such a bond to form, however, it requires a reformulation of how we conceive community. Rather than excluding excess to constitute a closed group, community must be a community of exiles and outsiders. This is why Lee shows Flipper as an exile at the end of the film, and it is also why he includes the relationship between Paulie and Orin (Tyra Ferrell). Though Paulie is Italian and is thoroughly ensconced in the Italian world, he asks Orin, who is black, to go out on a date. On his way to the date, Paulie's Italian acquaintances beat him up to punish him for the betrayal of their community, but he nonetheless goes to Orin's house to pick her up. When he arrives, she ushers him inside and begins to tend to his wounds. This moment of connection becomes possible because Paulie and Orin are willing to betray their communities and accept the permanent status of the excluded. At the end of the film, Paulie identifies himself with what exceeds his community and in this way makes possible a different form of community, a community of exiles. Throughout most of its running time, *Jungle Fever* emphasizes the dramatic costs of community, but the depiction of Paulie and Orin points toward another form of community that might be achieved without violent exclusivity. Paulie and Orin avoid the illusion of the threatening other necessary to the other communities visible in the film.

The exclusion that constitutes community functions on the basis of the idea that the other either threatens or has already stolen the community's enjoyment. But this enjoyment exists only insofar as the other threatens or steals it. There is no communal enjoyment without this threatening excessive other that serves to constitute it. Every community requires its excluded excess in order to function as a community, but at the same time, this excess undermines the community. This becomes apparent not only in *Jungle Fever* but throughout Spike Lee's work. What also becomes apparent, however, is the possibility for another type of community that doesn't rely on exclusion. It is the type of community that Paulie and Orin embody at the end of *Jungle Fever* or the various children at the end of *Malcolm X* create as they profess their identity with the ostracized Malcolm X. Rather than relying on exclusion, this type of community derives from it. It is thus completely insecure, existing without the stable boundaries of exclusive communities.

The idea of a community of outsiders or a community of excess manifests itself at the conclusion of Lee's film devoted to the Million Man March, *Get on the Bus*. Though the film recounts the pilgrimage that a group of men take to the Million Man March, it doesn't show them arriving. When the march takes place, Lee depicts it through television footage rather than re-creating the event for his film. He does this because the group itself never arrives at the march. Just as the bus comes to Washington, D.C. (where the march occurs), the oldest member of the group, Jeremiah (Ossie Davis), suffers a heart attack. They take him to the hospital, and some of the bus riders decide to stay with him while the others go on. But in the end, the rest of the group comes back to the hospital instead of attending the march.

The men don't form a community in which everyone has a sense of belonging and no antagonism exists. Hostility between them remains, and yet they come together through the act of missing the march. This is also how the film itself functions in relation to the spectator. Lee establishes the Million Man March as the central object in the film, and this object carries the promise of satisfaction for the men on the bus and for the spectator. But the bus never arrives at this object, and the men on the bus never become part of the community that forms at the march. The death of Jeremiah leaves them in the position of outsiders, and it is in this position that they can become a different type of community.

Though *Get on the Bus* seems initially to suggest the possibility of a traditional idea of community, its conclusion forces us to rethink this concept. Lee depicts the group of bus riders as an excess in relation to the Million Man March: they have tried to belong, but they cannot. Their exclusion provides a point at which they can come together, but it provides no point of identification. Unlike traditional communities that Lee critiques in *Crooklyn* and *Jungle Fever*, their community offers them no form of symbolic identity or authority figures with which to align themselves. In such a community, everyone is an outsider, and this is the ideal that Lee's cinema produces.

This vision of community finds its foremost realization in *Get on the Bus,* but there are other moments of it throughout Lee's cinema. One such moment occurs in *Summer of Sam,* a film that otherwise focuses on the paranoia and exclusion that constitutes a typical community. Though the Dead End Gang identifies Ritchie as the Son of Sam killer because of his failure to fit into the community, he does form a community of the excluded with Ruby (Jennifer Esposito), a woman from the neighborhood derided by Vinny and his friends as a "whore" for her sexual promiscuity. Both are outsiders, but rather than use opposition to the other as a means for entering the neighborhood community—Ritchie joining in the denunciation of Ruby's licentiousness, for instance—they embrace each other in their joint exclusion. When Vinny questions Ritchie's involvement with Ruby in light of her sexual past, Ritchie simply brushes off the question and indicates its unimportance. Here, community is possible through the embrace of exclusion rather than through the act of excluding. This contrast becomes clearest near the end of the film.

Just before the Dead End Gang beats Ritchie outside his house and concludes that they have captured the Son of Sam, we see Ruby and Ritchie sitting in Ritchie's garage apartment together as they have sex. Lee cuts between their sexual act and Vinny using drugs, and then between the sex and the Dead End Gang bringing Vinny to betray Ritchie. To arouse Vinny out of his drug-induced stupor, Joey, the leader of the Dead End Gang, punches him violently. The juxtaposition of Vinny's drug use and of this violence with the passion displayed by Ritchie and Ruby brings to light the two different possible forms of community. One excludes, and the other enjoys as excluded. But the end of the film reveals that the neighborhood community is not content to allow Ritchie and Ruby simply to enjoy their exclusion. They come to attack Ritchie because this excessive enjoyment constitutes a threat that makes their own community possible. Without the threat embodied by Ritchie and Ruby, the Dead End Gang and the entire neighborhood would have no sense of common identity. But nonetheless, *Summer of Sam* suggests another possibility through its depiction of Ritchie and Ruby. They are excessive in relation to the exclusive community, and they are satisfied to remain in this position of excess.

The depiction of a community of the excluded or a community of excess is the driving force behind Lee's war film *Miracle at St. Anna.* The

Beating up Ritchie at the end
of *Summer of Sam*.

film tells the story of black troops fighting in Italy during World War II, but it does so through the frame story of a police investigation. In 1983, a postal worker, Hector Negron (Laz Alonso), shoots a man from the Italian Resistance who betrayed them to the Germans. When a reporter, Tim Boyle (Joseph Gordon-Levitt), questions Negron in his jail cell, the film uses a flashback to recount the massacre that took place with the Buffalo Soldiers 92nd Infantry Division at the village of St. Anna. The flashback shows the exclusion that the Buffalo Soldiers suffer at the hands of the white Allied commanders, and it illustrates how a community forms out of this exclusion. The titular miracle is the formation of this community, which is the product of exclusion but doesn't itself rely on excluding anyone. In fact, it brings together black American soldiers, people from the Italian town, and even a German officer.

The flashback recounts an attack by the 92nd Division in which four members become trapped behind enemy lines in Italy after a white commander orders artillery fire on their position because he refuses to believe how far they have advanced. Lee shows the four surviving soldiers at odds with each other—struggling over the same woman, Renata (Valentia Cervi), for instance—but he also depicts the formation of a community among the Italians and them. One of the soldiers, Sam Train (Omar Benson Miller), even develops a language through tapping with a young Italian boy, Angelo (Matteo Sciabordi). This is a community of excess, of those who don't fit within either side in the war. But it also has a contingent and fleeting existence. When the Germans attack, aided by the betrayal of a resistance fighter, Rodolfo (Sergio Albelli), almost all of the members of this community die, including Renata and three of the four black soldiers. Only young Angelo and Hector Negron survive.

Hector's survival becomes possible only through an excessive act by a German commander. As Hector lies wounded on the streets of St. Anna, a German soldier comes to shoot him, but his commanding officer, Captain Eichholz (Christian Berkel), orders him away. Eichholz then hands Hector his own Luger, the weapon that Hector would years later use to kill Rodolfo in the American post office. With this act, Eichholz joins the community of excess that exists at St. Anna, even if only momentarily. He gives up his status as a German officer and identifies with those who don't fit within any social world in the film.

Though much of Lee's filmmaking represents an attack on the toxic nature of community and a critique of its reliance on exclusion, he also reveals the possibility for a form of community that avoids this reliance. The question concerning community in Lee's cinema centers around the position that we take up relative to excess. If we try to keep excess at bay and defend ourselves from it, we end up in an exclusive community. If instead we identify with excess, a community without exclusion can form. No one is excluded from the identification with excess, but such an identification doesn't provide respite from the trauma of our existential

The German solider's unexpected act
of kindness in *Miracle at St. Anna*.

groundlessness. The community of excess leaves its members without the sense of identity and security that traditional community offers.

Depictions of Antagonism

Community constitutes itself through exclusion to avoid suffocating on its own excess. But even exclusion cannot finally safeguard community from itself. The ostracized other makes possible the communal bond, but this bond itself remains tenuous. It is always a fractured bond. Community forms not only through the exclusion of its own excess but also through the disavowal of the antagonism that constantly threatens to split the community apart. The community's excess appears not only through what it excludes but also through the internal opposition that it necessarily engenders. There is always too much community or too much society, and the testament to this excess is the antagonism that no society is able to avoid.

The chief task of ideology is the obfuscation of antagonism. When subjects become aware of the antagonism that animates their social existence, they gain insight into the precarious nature of the social arrangement itself and the absence of any ontological foundation for these arrangements. The fight against social injustice and for equality necessarily stems from a grasp of the antagonism that ideology tries to hide. On the whole, cinema disseminates ideological fantasies that hide antagonism. This occurs primarily through the creation of a concluding romantic union assuring spectators that conflicts are complementary rather than antagonistic.

Antagonistic conflicts harbor no solution. The best that one can do is embrace the irreducibility of the antagonism and view it as constitutive of the social or romantic relation that it threatens to destroy. This is the path that psychoanalysis takes up toward antagonism, and it is why Freud concludes near the end of his life that most analysis is probably interminable. Patients enter analysis looking for the solution to the antagonism that troubles them, but no analyst can lead them toward its solution. This is obviously a very unappealing position, which is perhaps why only a small percentage of therapists are psychoanalysts. No one wants to believe that what threatens one's relations is at the same time their condition of possibility. As a result, film, as a popular medium, tends to take the opposite tack and to proffer fantasies about the overcoming of antagonism.

In these fantasies, the antagonism of romance of the individual and the society or even of racial opposition becomes ameliorated through an image of two sides fitting together as complements. The predominant image of complementarity is the male and female, and this is the image that cinema utilizes more than any other. We see a paradigmatic case in Rob Reiner's *When Harry Met Sally* (1989), where the obsessive and sexually restrained Sally ends up with her complementary partner in the carefree and libidinous Harry. Though the entire film displays the antagonism in their relation, the conclusion reveals that what appeared as an antagonism is actually a complementary opposition. This is the fantasmatic dimension of the film, a dimension that it shares with many productions in the history of cinema.

The difference between antagonism and complementary opposition is that the former offers no prospect of resolution. An antagonism involves two opposing positions that do not even recognize the same ground on which they exist, and as a consequence, they cannot be fitted together. In Marx's example of antagonism, class antagonism, the proletariat and the bourgeoisie do not simply take a different political stance but instead see two fundamentally different political terrains. For the proletariat, society is the arena of class struggle, while for the bourgeoisie, it is an organic whole in which everyone has an equal opportunity in the free market and in which there are no foundational divisions. In contrast, two competing positions in a complementary opposition accept the same terrain as the ground for their dispute—like the Democratic and Republican parties in the contemporary United States, for whom global capitalism constitutes their shared ground, and their argument consists of different ways of comporting oneself on this ground.

Spike Lee's commitment to social excess leads him to focus on antagonism, which places him outside the prevailing filmmaking practices in the history of cinema. Though Lee is a thoroughly political filmmaker, his films never offer political solutions. This becomes most pronounced at the end of one of his most political films. *Do the Right Thing* concludes with a white police force murdering a black man and a group of black citizens destroying the white-owned pizzeria in the aftermath. Lee leaves two quotations on the screen at the end: one from Martin Luther King advocating nonviolent resistance, and the other from Malcolm X calling for resistance "by any means necessary." He doesn't endorse either but simply shows the two alternatives.

The idea inherent in this ending is not that we must opt for one or the other but that the situation itself makes it impossible to decide. Because the situation always exceeds its own terms, Lee shows, it is impossible to find a clear resolution. If we respond within the terms of the situation, as Martin Luther King suggests, we risk allowing injustice to triumph, but if we respond excessively, as Malcolm X suggests, we risk becoming like those we are struggling against. Lee's other political films take up a similar position: there is no easy answer when one confronts the excesses of a political situation.

Do the Right Thing generates sympathy for most of its characters and the arguments that they advance, and at the same time, it undermines these characters as political actors. Buggin' Out has a genuine objection to the absence of any black heroes on the wall of the local pizzeria, owned by an Italian, Sal. And yet Buggin' Out appears to protest just for the sake of protesting, and other black characters make light of his political campaign. Mookie (Spike Lee) appears justified in his decision to throw a trashcan through the window of the pizzeria, an act that occasions the restaurant's destruction by the neighborhood. But Mookie's act doesn't lead to any political awakening or genuine transformation. Even Sal, whose use of the word "nigger" begins the overt conflict, is sympathetic throughout most of the film and seems genuinely to care for the neighborhood and for his customers. In fact, Dan Flory rightly calls Sal a "sympathetic racist," one so sympathetic that "many white viewers tend not to notice or acknowledge the racist dimension of Sal's character" (*Philosophy* 47). Other than the police officers who kill Radio Raheem, there are no uncomplicated villains or heroes.

One comes away from *Do the Right Thing* with a clear sense of the political imperative stated explicitly in the film's title. After viewing the film, the spectator must try to "do the right thing." But it is not at all obvious what this entails. This question befuddles the critic Norman Denzin and many others. Denzin asks, "But what is the right thing? Right for whom? Nonviolence appears to be questionable tool for social change. However, it is not clear that violence offers a viable alternative" (111). The film does offer certain explicit negative definitions: avoid the use of ethnic slurs, guard against racist stereotyping, and above all, don't permit the strangulation of innocent black teens by a brutal white police force. Beyond these obvious strictures, the politics of the film are not self-evident, even for the attentive spectator.

Perhaps this is why certain critics have taken Lee to task not for being an overtly political filmmaker but for failing to be political enough. Two of the most prominent figures of this line of attack are Victoria E. Johnson and Douglas Kellner. According to Johnson (who appreciates Lee's use of music in the film), Lee fails on the level of politics by refusing to take up fully the oppositional voice that he unleashes. What results is, in Johnson's idiom, a "conflicted" politics: "Lee's 'politicized' voice is most conflicted . . . as his films grant expression to voices that are typically marginalized in relation to the mainstream, only for those oppositions to be subsumed by larger commodification practices that recoup them for popular sale as black history and politics" (70). The problem with Lee's political voice lies in the conflict that it cannot overcome. Politics, as Johnson sees it, must mark out a distinct position rather than simply depict an irreducible conflict.

Douglas Kellner is even more open in his critique of Lee's failure to show possibilities for positive political action and his tendency to

No clear villains in *Do the Right Thing* except the police.

undermine those that have been successful. Kellner credits Lee with his depiction of racial dynamics on an individual level, but this never translates into a genuine political project. This absence of such a project hampers the political effectiveness of *Do the Right Thing*. According to Kellner, "Lee presents racism in personal and individualist terms as hostility among members of different groups, thus failing to illuminate the causes and structures of racism. Moreover, the film denigrates political action, caricaturing collective action and the tactic of the economic boycott, which served the Civil Rights movement so well" (82). Kellner indicts the film precisely for its inability to transcend the persistence of antagonism.

But what Kellner, Johnson, and other critics view as the failure of *Do the Right Thing*, we should count as its success. To be sure, it is not the standard political film that highlights a social injustice and shows the path to its eradication. Instead, Lee draws attention to the antagonism between black and white (which is also—or initially—a class antagonism) that continues to bedevil American society and the world. He also renders visible the antagonism that haunts all possible political responses to racial injustice. Neither the problem itself nor the political remedies admit a solution, but the result is not political acquiescence to the ruling conditions. Instead, one must "fight the power," but one must do so through the avowal of antagonism and not its repression.

The failure of progressive politics lies in this direction. It has attempted to solve antagonism rather than embracing it, and Lee's cinema points us toward this embrace. This does not make for easily extracted political messages or for uplifting films that send spectators straight to the barricades. The political task envisioned by Lee's films involves the struggle within as much as the struggle against the external enemy, because the external enemy is always ultimately a form of the enemy within. In other words, to address the racial antagonism that divides American society, one must also confront the antagonism that divides black from black or white from white. This is why Lee makes *School Daze* before *Do the Right Thing*: the latter is unquestionably the more important film, but the former sets the stage for it by taking up antagonism among black characters without any overt white interference.

After the credit sequence that features black-and-white stills of figures from African American history, *School Daze*, a musical detailing racial politics at the historically black Mission College, begins with a scene of Dap (Laurence Fishburne) leading a protest for divestment from South Africa on the steps of the campus administration building. As Dap articulates the shame of the black college's continued economic support of the apartheid regime, a group of fraternity pledges—the Gamma Dogs of Gamma Phi Gamma—come and disrupt the protest. A confrontation ensues between Julian (Giancarlo Esposito), the leader of the fraternity, and Dap, which ends only with the intervention of the student-body president, who pleads for peace. With this initial scene, Lee establishes the fundamental antagonism that marks the film—between the apolitical and the politically committed, between the fraternity or sorority members and the nonmembers, between the assimilationists and the Africanists, and between the light-skinned black characters and the dark-skinned. This antagonism is multilayered and impossible to resolve. There is no possible common ground between the opposed positions because each, as the film reveals, is at odds with itself. *School Daze* illustrates the difference between antagonism and complementary opposition by underlining the self-division that animates the opposed positions. Dap and his friends disagree over their political commitment and their willingness to disrupt classes at the school, while Julian betrays his girlfriend and sorority member Jane Toussaint (Tisha Campbell Martin) toward the end of the film. The two sides reveal an internal opposition that is altogether as bitter as their opposition to the other side, and this reflects the politics of the film as a whole.

Lee's film about a historically black college does not concern itself with the white racism that necessitated such colleges and that continues to inform their existence. Instead, it focuses on the antagonism within the black college itself. And then within that antagonism, Lee shows how each opposing side is divided against itself. This complex structure results from his devotion to the idea of antagonism and to an understanding of the role that antagonism plays in the political act. Politics for Lee is not the overcoming of antagonism and the achievement of mutual recognition but the recognition that we cannot overcome antagonism. Even where we would anticipate and welcome its resolution, antagonism retains its power over us.

The antagonism between the two groups becomes especially evident during a fantasmatic musical number that occurs during a confrontation in a campus hallway between the light-skinned black women who belong to a sorority and the dark-skinned women who don't. They label each other with various slurs, including "wannabe" and "jigaboo," their primary terms for the women on the other side. What is remarkable about this conflict is that it occurs within a musical number, often the point in a film where conflicts between characters are resolved.

The number performed during this confrontation clearly alludes to a musical from the 1970s set in high school rather than college—*Grease* (Randal Kleiser, 1978). Lee makes this allusion apparent by setting the number in a beauty parlor, even though the argument between the two groups takes place on the college campus. This shift in setting is striking, though we only recognize it as fantasmatic after the fact, when the number ends and the film returns to the conflict in the hallway. In *Grease,* the young women overcome their internecine conflicts for a few minutes while they sing "Beauty School Dropout" in a beauty parlor. Here, despite the ill will between Rizzo (Stockard Channing) and Sandy (Olivia Newton-John), the women come together in the musical number that affirms their support for Frenchy (Didi Conn), who is the song's titular failure. There is no such affirmation in the number from *School Daze.*

The title of the number itself suggests opposition rather than resolution. The women sing "Straight and Nappy," which highlights the character of their insults against each other. The light-skinned women attack the dark-skinned women for their nappy hair, while the latter attack the former for the straight hair associated with whiteness. Lee shoots the number to emphasize the opposition: the light-skinned women are dressed in silver, while the dark-skinned women are in red. Lee moves the camera forward through a series of close-ups that show the women confronting each other face to face. As the camera passes them, they turn away, and another opposed pair appears in close-up. In contrast to *Grease* and other musicals, the number here serves to separate rather than unite.

Though the musical number presents the opposition straightforwardly and doesn't openly take sides, there can be little doubt where the film's sympathies lie. Not only does the film begin with Dap's convincing argument for divestment, but he is also the most appealing character in the film. Though his commitment to political activity produces a quarrel with his girlfriend, Rachel Meadows (Kyme), when he balks at her decision to join a sorority, his quick about-face after some reflection sustains him as an attractive figure. Even when he errs like he does by berating Rachel for her decision to pledge, he does so from a sincere political commitment. Julian, his primary antagonist in the film and spokesperson for the assimilationists, garners none of the sympathy that flows to Dap. In his first appearance, he mistreats pledges—forcing them to act like dogs and to refer to him as "Dean Big Brother Almight-tee"— and continues to do so throughout the film. Toward the end, he decides to break up with Jane, his girlfriend, but rather than simply end the relationship, he prostitutes her, asking her to prove her love for him and the fraternity by having sex with a new member, Half Pint (Spike Lee). After Jane acquiesces in an attempt to save their relationship, Julian leaves her and uses the act that he ordered as the justification. Here, the dramatic contrast between the political and ethical Dap and the white-identified Julian becomes fully apparent.

The idea of antagonism does not imply that both sides are equal and that we must try to meld them together to come up with the proper position. In an antagonism, one must take sides, but one must take the side that avows and sustains the antagonism as such. Within every antagonistic structure, one side sees the irreducible antagonism, while the other side sees two complementary oppositions that might be reconciled with each other. The former position in *School Daze* belongs to Dap, while the latter is identified with Julian. Dap understands that the temptation to fit in with white society and to accept its strictures (like fraternities and sororities) will continue to create an antagonism for black Americans, and yet he fights against this temptation. Julian, on the contrary, believes in the possibility of full integration into white American society, which would eliminate Dap's position altogether and put an end to the antagonism. In this sense, the respective attitudes toward antagonism on each side are asymmetrical: one side believes in the impossibility of overcoming it, while the other side never really avows antagonism at all. This is what places *School Daze* on the side of Dap, despite his faults.

Dap grasps the antagonism because he is the figure of excess in the film. His excessive commitment to his political activity puts him in conflict with Julian, with the school administration, and even with his girlfriend Rachel. But this excess is also what makes him into an appealing character. The other characters in the film do their best to avoid antagonism and to play down its effects whenever possible, but Dap accentuates it and proclaims its existence. His own excess as a character enables him to identify the antagonism that results from excess and that other characters blind themselves to.

But the ending of *School Daze* seems to belie its focus on antagonism. After he hears that Julian has encouraged his girlfriend Jane to have sex with Half Pint, the virginal new member of the fraternity, Dap loses control and runs across the campus screaming "Wake up!" multiple times and ringing the campus bell despite the early hour. When he does this the first time, he runs across the middle of the campus green and stares directly into the camera before yelling, "Wake up!" At this point, the film moves from indirect to direct address, and the remaining moments function as admonitions to the spectator as much as to the other characters within the diegetic reality of the film. In the final scene, Dap's antagonist Julian walks up to him and looks him in the eyes. They stand face to face, and then both turn toward the camera as Dap says, "Please, wake up." The image of the two of them transforms into a black-and-white photograph, just like those used in the opening credit sequence—and alluding to the famous photograph of Martin Luther King and Malcolm X that plays such an important role in *Do the Right Thing*. Though Julian is no Martin Luther King (or even a Booker T. Washington), he does nonetheless sustain one side of the antagonism at Mission College. As the photograph forms from the film image, an alarm rings and reminds the spectator once again of Dap's repeated admonition, "Wake up!"

Just as *Do the Right Thing* never alerts the spectator as to where its political sympathies lie relative to the opposition between Martin Luther King and Malcolm X, *School Daze* provides no definitive way of reading Dap's insistence that we "wake up." Dap is the more sympathetic character, but in the final scene a rapprochement, triggered by Dap's call, appears to take place between him and Julian. Dap begins shouting "Wake up!" when his cousin Half Pint comes to his dorm room in the morning after he had sex with Jane at Julian's urging. This prostituting of one's girlfriend so offends Dap that he feels compelled to make a public statement, even though this statement remains ambiguous. "Wake up!" must be understood through Dap's insistence on antagonism during the rest of the film but also through the manner in which Lee decides to shoot the final scene.

Julian walks up to Dap and apparently reconciles with him at the end of the film, but the reconciliation still sustains an antagonism. Julian doesn't say anything and simply looks Dap in the face. When they turn together to address the camera directly, they do not, as we might expect, speak in unison. Only Dap says, "Please, wake up." Even at a point of agreement between the two, the antagonism persists and will persist, but it is possible to wake up to the antagonism itself rather than trying to eliminate it. This is what *School Daze* pleads for in its concluding scene, and this is what animates *Do the Right Thing* as well. By siding with excess, we can sustain the antagonism that gives vitality to our existence at the same time as it threatens that existence.

Within contemporary ideology, the one site that always appears free of antagonism is the family. The family provides constant support and psychic nourishment, even if the social order leaves one isolated and alone. Most films proffer this ideology wholeheartedly, from mainstream Hollywood films like Jason Reitman's *Up in the Air* (2009) or David O. Russell's *The Fighter* (2010) to independent films like Jonathan Dayton and Valerie Faris's *Little Miss Sunshine* (2006) and Lisa Cholodenko's *The Kids Are Alright* (2010). Even when such films begin by showing the family as dysfunctional or calling the familial bond into question, they conclude with an affirmation that heals any sense of antagonism. Antagonism exists in these films and in a multitude of others as a barrier that the familial bond can surmount and thereby eliminate. The fact that the family functions as an ultimate bedrock even in films that take up a critical attitude toward it suggests its ideological centrality. One can question all aspects of the social order today, but one cannot doubt the foundational status of the family.

But Spike Lee's commitment to the idea of antagonism is such that even his semiautobiographical film about the family, *Crooklyn*, reveals it as riven with antagonism. In the film, antagonism does not simply pull the family apart; it also holds the family together. As Lee sees it, without the antagonism between Woody and Carolyn, or the antagonism among the brothers Clinton (Carlton Williams), Wendell (Sharif Rashed), Joseph (Tse-Mach Washington), Nate (Christopher Knowings), and the sister Troy (Zelda Harris), there would be no familial bond at all. Family love is inextricable from the antagonism that threatens to break up the family in *Crooklyn*.

The relation to antagonism separates *Crooklyn* from films like *The Fighter* and *Little Miss Sunshine*. Even in films where the actual family ceases to exist, a symbolic one often forms to take its place and provide a place where antagonism can be surmounted, as in a film like *The Goonies* (Richard Donner, 1985). In all these other films, characters realize that they depend on family members and cannot succeed without the family as a whole. In contrast, *Crooklyn* places the emphasis on the irreducibility of the conflicts that inhere within the family. Carolyn's commitment to providing for the family runs up against Woody's dedication to the purity of his art, and Woody's concert forces his son Clinton to miss seeing the New York Knicks win the NBA championship, an event that he had been dreaming about for months. Among the children themselves, Lee depicts a constant antagonism: they fight about what they'll watch on television, mock each other, and even on one occasion steal from each other. But as the film makes clear, these conflicts are constitutive of the bond.

This becomes apparent when Troy goes to Virginia to stay with her relatives. Uncle Clem (Norman Matlock) and Aunt Song (Frances Foster) and cousin Viola (Patriece Nelson) live in a seemingly harmonious family relation, an apparent ideal that contrasts with the Carmichael family in Brooklyn. It is family life without the antagonism that haunts the Carmichael household. But at the same time, the cost of the absence of antagonism becomes fully evident as Lee explores the family relations of the Virginia relatives. The relations are harmonious because Aunt Song rules the family absolutely. Neither Clem nor Viola challenges the authority of Aunt Song, and when Troy does so, Aunt Song responds with authoritarianism. Due to Aunt Song's absolute control, the bond between Clem, Viola, and herself is entirely absent.

Family life without antagonism is possible, *Crooklyn* suggests, but it is a life without any familial bond. The contrast between Brooklyn and Virginia is one between an antagonistic family and a harmonious one. The former creates the possibility of a familial bond, while the latter paradoxically militates against it. Even in the domain where contemporary ideology figures antagonism as entirely absent, the family, Lee's films show an entity rife with antagonism. Rather than lament antagonism in the family, however, Lee celebrates it, and it is this celebration that animates *Crooklyn*.

The Million Man March on October 16, 1995, had as its aim not the celebration of antagonism but the expression of unity. The march organizer Benjamin Chavis and keynote speaker Louis Farrakhan designed the event as a moment for black men to overcome internal conflicts and unite in their own self-defense. According to the "Million Man March/ Day of Absence Mission Statement" written by Maulana Karenga, "It is both an example and encouragement of operational unity; unity in diversity, unity without uniformity and unity on principle and in practice for the greater good" (142). Though this statement acknowledges that diversity must exist within the unity of the march, it nonetheless proclaims the possibility of a unity that would overcome antagonism. Spike Lee's 1996 film *Get on the Bus* centers around the Million Man March, but rather than echo the spirit of unity that this event hoped to foster, Lee uses the collective action as an occasion to present the unrelenting presence of antagonism even amid the most determined efforts to create wholeness.

The decision to create a film in the wake of the Million Man March appears strange when we examine Lee's propensity for revealing antagonism. But as with *Crooklyn*, here he takes an arena where everyone expects antagonism to evaporate and exposes its persistence. Lee doesn't do this simply to upset cherished convictions about unity and wholeness but out of a sense of the emancipatory power of antagonism. If we can recognize antagonism at points where we imagine wholeness, we can emancipate ourselves from the ideological trap that wholeness represents and attach ourselves instead to a bond forged through antagonism rather than through its repression.

Get on the Bus depicts a busload of black men traveling from Los Angeles to the march in Washington, D.C., and throughout the trip, antagonistic relations appear between different groups of characters on the bus and even among those who are taking the trip together. After the opening credits, the first scene of the film shows a father and son walking on the sidewalk handcuffed together. The handcuffs provide an objective correlative of the relationship between the two (and between all the bus riders): they are physically united but psychically at odds. The son, Smooth (De'Aundre Bonds), doesn't want to get on the bus or even be near his father, while the father, Evan Thomas (Thomas Jefferson Byrd), believes that the bus trip and march will provide an opportunity for him to atone for his earlier absence from his son's life.

The hostility between the two manifested in this early scene continues throughout the film and even occurs on the most fundamental level: they cannot agree on the son's name. The father wants to call his son "Junior" or "Evan Junior," but the son insists on the name that his friends use, "Smooth." The antagonism culminates in Smooth's attempt to run away after the fellow riders convince Evan to remove the court-mandated handcuffs. Though the father and son explain themselves to each other after the failed escape, there is no solution to the antagonism between them, which results not so much from their individual failures as from the structural positions that they inhabit.

In comparison with the other riders on the bus, however, the fraught relationship between father and son seems almost ideal. The film chronicles a gay couple in the midst of breaking up, rabidly homophobic men confronting the gay couple, a dark-skinned man impugning the blackness of a man with a white mother, a cop whose police-officer father was killed by gang violence facing a former gang member who admits to several killings, and so on. Lee does not offer any resolution to these antagonisms: the couple does not get back together; the homophobic men do not become suddenly enlightened; the dark-skinned man does not change his view of the white mother; and the cop does not forgive the violence of the former gang member, despite the latter's current work in helping at-risk youth in South Central Los Angeles. In fact, the final interaction between Gary (Robert Guenveur Smith), the cop, and Jamal (Gabriel Casseus), the former gang member, involves Gary pushing Jamal against a wall and promising to spare no effort in bringing him to justice for his past crimes.

The film does not simply depict multiple variations of black masculinity that exist alongside each other. Difference implies the possibility for reconciliation within the unified whole, and such reconciliation does not exist within the universe of *Get on the Bus*. Nonetheless, this is how the critic S. Craig Watkins views the film. He acknowledges particular differences but understands these differences coming together within a larger unity: "Even as *Get on the Bus* strives to make the case that black men make up a complex mix of identities, values, and experience, it also maintains that they are bound together by the powerful history of race and gender in America" (154). Watkins's statement illustrates perfectly the compatibility between particular difference and collective unity. In Lee's film, however, the different identities do not exist alongside each other but in an antagonistic relation. The gay men confront the homophobic men, or the police officer attacks the confessed cop killer. In each of these instances and others, the identities cannot be "bound together" because they imply the nonexistence of the opposing position. Lee carefully shows antagonism rather than difference, and antagonism, in contrast to difference, eliminates any possible reconciliation or unity.

In addition to these outbreaks of antagonism among the black men going to the march, the film also details the antagonism between black and white that occasions the march in the first place. When the bus that the men are riding breaks down midway through the trip, another bus comes to take them the rest of the way. This new bus, unlike the first one, has a white driver, who is Jewish. The men on the bus find a white driver inappropriate for the Million Man March, and Rick (Richard Belzer), the white driver, feels uncomfortable in this position himself. Though Rick expresses his colorblindness, he also tells George (Charles S. Dutton), the trip leader, that he can't continue on as the driver. Rick uses the keynote speaker Louis Farrakhan's anti-Semitism as his reason for abandoning the bus, but it is clear that Rick's discomfort extends beyond this when he brings up the problems of affirmative action and O. J. Simpson's guilt as further reasons for being unable to drive the bus. Through the character of Rick, we see how racism appears beneath the veneer of colorblindness, and the film allows for no possibility that the bus trip might lead Rick to overcome his largely unconscious racism. In fact, the trip and the interracial contact that it provides exacerbate this racism. Rick simply walks off into the night with his bags and leaves George to drive the bus alone.

Not only does the film not offer any opportunity for Rick to transcend his racism and experience a connection with the men on the bus, but it exposes the falsity of reconciliation when it does occur. If the company found out that Rick abandoned the bus due to his racism, he would lose his job, so he asks George to cover for him with the company. Rick puts out his hand to George seeking agreement, and the film shows George reluctantly shaking Rick's hand after a few seconds without a reaction.

It appears as if George will not take Rick's hand, but when he does, the lack of any connection between them is evident. George agrees to help Rick even though he has no relationship with him. Though the gesture of shaking hands suggests the overcoming of antagonism, *Get on the Bus* reveals that it can easily leave the antagonism perfectly intact or even deepen it, as it does when Rick pressures George into the handshake just after communicating his own racism.

Like the relationship between George and Rick, none of the antagonistic relations on the bus find a resolution during the trip or at the Million Man March itself. Jeremiah's heart attack prevents the riders from attending the march, and the community that forms after his death doesn't eliminate the antagonisms. But this does not indicate that the film is ultimately pessimistic about the possibility for changed social relations. The first image of the film is a handcuff that the camera moves through, and the final image is a pair of abandoned handcuffs, which suggest that some form of emancipation has taken place.

In Lee's cinema, emancipation does not occur through the overcoming of antagonism or through the attainment of reconciliation. His refusal to offer this vision of emancipation riles numerous critics. For instance, in *Reel to Real*, bell hooks takes Lee to task for his failure to depict what she calls a "liberatory reconciliation" in his first feature. She says, "Even though filmmaker Spike Lee may have intended to portray a radical new image of black female sexuality, *She's Gotta Have It* reinforces and perpetuates old norms overall. Positively the film does show us the nature of black male-female power struggles, the contradictions, the craziness, and that is an important new direction. Yet it is the absence of compelling liberatory reconciliation that undermines the progressive radical potential of the film" (235). Sharon Willis furthers this line of critique. For her, Lee's failure is also a failure to indicate the possibility of overcoming antagonism. In *High Contrast*, she notes, "It is as if Lee were fixated in an oedipal universe structured by father-son and mother-daughter dramas, where no real cross-gender exchange occurs" (187). Both hooks and Willis indict Lee for remaining within antagonism rather than finding a way to surmount it. From their point of view, this indicates an absence of political possibilities in his cinema.

But Lee asks us to change our idea of politics and of emancipation. Hollywood has historically portrayed change through the image of overcoming antagonism. This image most often occurs in romance or action films, though it also provides the model in explicitly political films. From *Gentleman's Agreement* (Elia Kazan, 1947) and *The Defiant Ones* (Stanley Kramer, 1958) to *The Color Purple* (Steven Spielberg, 1985) and *Mississippi Burning* (Alan Parker, 1988), Hollywood identifies political transformation with overcoming antagonism. This might involve eliminating a character that embodies attitudes that create antagonism or characters overcoming their own inclinations. In whatever form it takes, however, this trajectory is almost ubiquitous and determines not only Hollywood's politics but also the way that we tend to think of any political change. Even Marxism views the proletarian revolution as a way of ending class antagonism in society by transcending class altogether.

Spike Lee's vision of political change is completely different. He doesn't stress antagonism in his films so that we might recognize it and then overcome it; his cinema makes clear that there is no way out of antagonism. As a result, the only possibility for political change or for emancipation involves identifying with the antagonism rather than trying to overcome it. By identifying with the antagonism, we align ourselves with the excess of the social order and free ourselves from its restrictions. It is precisely Lee's refusal to present the possibility of transcending antagonism—what hooks, Willis, and others criticize—that establishes a different form of political transcendence.

No Outside

The premise of all political acts is the idea that change is possible, that a collective transcendence of the current social conditions can occur. And yet, the idea of transcendence, as Lee's films repeatedly show, leads to a politically crippling paranoid vision of the world, in which those in the transcendent position have a privileged relation to enjoyment. The political filmmaker such as Spike Lee must find a way to navigate this paradox: transcendence is at once the linchpin of the political act and its ruination. Lee manages to create political films that avoid both pure immanence and transcendence through consistent turns to excess. Excess emerges not through the transcendence of immanence but through a surplus of immanence itself. That is to say, there is always too much immanence, and it is precisely this that Lee's films aim to capture and cultivate as the terrain of political contestation. The capacity for depicting excess through the cinema derives from a transformation of the social order that occurs with modernity. The onset of modernity and the disappearance of the transcendent sovereign changes the structural constitution of society in a way not often noticed. The excess formerly embodied by the transcendent sovereign enters into the social immanence. In *The Royal Remains,* Eric Santner describes this process as one that requires a rethinking of the typical narrative of modernity. He notes, "It becomes misleading to analyze the core crisis of modernity under the sign of loss, of losing our access to transcendence . . . ; the 'death of God' would seem rather to concern a fateful process of becoming stuck with an excess, a *too-muchness,* within the space of immanence. It is not simply that we cannot come to terms with our lot as finite human subjects but rather that our finitude itself suffers from a kind of intrinsic dysfunction, a lack of measure and balance" (82). With modernity and the toppling of transcendent authority, the social field itself becomes excessive and ceases to operate smoothly. Excess loses its designated position in sovereign authority and becomes ubiquitous. One encounters it in the passion of the revolutionary, the brutality of the police officer, the intensity of the lover, the aggression of the racist, and even the zeal of workers for their jobs. This excess, what Santner calls "too-muchness," produces a territory within the social field of immanence from which a filmmaker can launch a form of politics that avoids pure immanence and transcendence, and this is the politics of Spike Lee's cinema.

The field of immanence created in a Lee film appears most directly in the film's setting. Lee often confines his films to a restricted location that the characters never leave. In *Do the Right Thing,* this sense of restriction is more pronounced than in any other Lee film: the action never leaves the one-block area in Brooklyn where the film takes place. Even *Crooklyn,* another film that utilizes a confined Brooklyn neighborhood, allows viewers some respite when the family travels to visit relatives, and *School Daze* permits brief trips off the college campus to the local town. But *Do the Right Thing* never leaves the Brooklyn neighborhood, despite the fact that Sal and his sons live elsewhere, in an Italian neighborhood. The characters who do go home during the film, like Mookie, live within the one-block radius. The heat that permeates the neighborhood on the summer day appears like an effect of the confined setting. With nowhere to escape, the heat generated by the individuals themselves becomes suffocating, and the hostility that manifests itself seems to be the product of the absence of any outside. With nowhere to go, characters inevitably collide with each other.

Though *Do the Right Thing* stresses the absence of any outside, it also emphasizes the various modes of excess that are possible within the field of immanence. The racist excess of Sal and Pino, who unleash derogatory epithets directed at the residents of the neighborhood, are examples of momentary transcendence within the confines of the setting. The sexual experience between Mookie and Tina (Rosie Perez) also exceeds the situation, though in a wholly different way. When they rub ice over each other's body, the cooling effect of the ice indicates a point where they escape the heat, and the sexual arousal also transports both beyond the confines of their world and even their troubled relationship. The film uses the narrow setting to illustrate how the narrowest space exceeds itself and offers the subject the possibility of a genuine act. This is what occurs when Mookie throws the trashcan through the window of Sal's Pizzeria at the end of the film.

The confined world of *Do the Right Thing*. |

At first glance, Mookie's act appears as the product of the context in which it occurs. The crowd seeks vengeance for the death of Radio Raheem, and Mookie's gesture is nothing but the response to this pressure. But this is to underestimate the complexity of Mookie's act. By throwing the trashcan through the window, Mookie simultaneously protests Sal's racism and the death of Radio Raheem that Sal ultimately produced, and yet he also directs the crowd's rage against Sal's property and not his person. It transcends the field of immanence without being transcendent.

Ironically, Lee's two films that depict excessive immanence most insightfully are two of his least overtly political films. In *25th Hour* and *Inside Man,* Lee relates one story of a man's last day of freedom before seven years in prison and another of an inventive bank heist. *25th Hour* focuses on an excess within our finite temporality: even though Monty Brogan only has one day of free life left, the limit seems to lead to possibilities that he otherwise would not have had. The finitude of his time gives him an excess within time where time ceases to hold sway. The title of the film also indicates this relationship to time: instead of labeling Monty's one day with the number of hours that it contains, Lee adds an additional hour to the title, suggesting that each finite unit of time has more time within it than we can count. The temporal limit that Monty's situation places on his life has the ironic effect of making evident the excessive time that he has within that limit.

The excessive time that Monty has within his day manifests itself through the film's form. Scenes from Monty's past—such as the drug bust that led to his seven-year prison sentence and the moment that he met his girlfriend Naturelle—appear within the single day in which the film takes place. There is no clear signal that these are flashbacks. Instead, they reveal how the temporal limit that the film establishes exceeds itself. This becomes even more evident in the repetition of several brief moments that occur throughout the day.

The first of these repetitions takes place when Monty greets his old friend Jacob Elinsky (Philip Seymour Hoffman) while the latter is teaching his high-school class. They hug, and then Lee shows the same gesture a second time. Lee employs this technique a second time when Agent Flood (Isaiah Whitlock Jr.) finds drugs in Monty's apartment. Twice we see Agent Flood say the word "shit" in an exaggerated and elongated fashion (an excessive gesture that he employs again when he returns as the same character in a completely different context in *She Hate Me*). This adds emphasis to the sense of doom that hangs over Monty and removes this moment that changes his life from all temporality. Even though Monty has a limited amount of time, he has an infinite amount of moments during that time that he experiences without any sense of temporality. At the key points in Monty's single remaining day of freedom, events repeat themselves, suggesting an excess that transcends the time limit imposed by the authorities.

Monty's concern for excess is evident in the first scene of the film, which itself is excessive because it is the only one that occurs outside of the day before Monty will go to jail. Over the opening production-company credit on a black screen, the audio track includes sounds of violence being done to a dog. The first shot of the film shows Monty and Kostya (Tony Siragusa) driving in New York and stopping where the injured dog is lying. At first, Monty asks for a gun to shoot the dog to end its misery, but when the dog shows liveliness, he decides to rescue it and places it in the trunk of his car. Though it bites him on the neck, the next scene depicting Monty with the same dog sometime later reveals that he has decided to keep the dog rather than drop it at the animal hospital, as he stated he would. The dog is left for dead, and Monty adopts it because of his concern for this excess.

Not only does this opening scene stick out temporally from the rest of the film, but it also has no direct function within the filmic narrative. Nonetheless, Lee begins with it to signal the importance that excess will have within the film, despite the strict confines of the narrative. The dog is excessive within the diegesis, and the scene involving the dog exceeds the formal limit that the film itself establishes. The narrative confines itself to a field of immanence, but that field has excesses just like those in *Do the Right Thing*.

Inside Man performs a similar operation in terms of space. Even though it represents a turn to genre filmmaking, Lee manages to manipulate the generic conventions to construct a commentary on excess. There have obviously been many variations on the heist film throughout the history of cinema, but the structure of *Inside Man* carves out a new path while remaining firmly within the genre. The film does this in a number of ways: the thieves rob the bank but leave all the money; they hide themselves among the hostages rather than separating themselves; the getaway for the leader involves remaining inside the bank rather than leaving it; and the interviews with the freed hostages are interspersed throughout the depiction of the robbery. While the first three reformulations of the heist film occur on the level of content, the final one is a formal device. What each has in common is the elimination of transcendence and the alignment of excess with immanence.

The heist film takes as its fundamental premise the attempt at escape or transcendence. Thieves attempt a heist to get out of the confines of their present condition—usually by trying to obtain some form of wealth to become rich. Many heist films detail the failure of this fantasy and thus implicitly suggest the impossibility of any transcendence. This occurs famously in Jules Dassin's *Du rififi chez les hommes* (1955), Stanley Kubrick's *The Killing* (1956), Joseph Sargent's *The Taking of Pelham One Two Three* (1974), Michael Mann's *Heat* (1995), and many others. In Mann's film, for instance, the leader of the thieves, Neil McCauley (Robert De Niro), foils his otherwise successful escape by seeking revenge even against his own better judgment. In most heist films, however, the quest for transcendence succeeds, and the thieves, like Charlie Croker (Mark Wahlberg) and Stella Bridger (Charlize Theron) in F. Gary Gray's *The Italian Job* (2003), pull off the heist. Whatever the final result, it is the quest for transcendence that animates the heist film as a genre.

Given the association of the heist film with the idea of transcendence, Lee's decision to make a film in this genre is peculiar, and to make a successful heist film, he must radically modify the genre. Unlike Dassin and Kubrick, Lee doesn't want to show the impossibility of any escape or the reducibility of subjects to their situations. But unlike Gray, neither does he seek to envision the possibility of transcendence through the heist. Hence, he must create a heist film in which escape occurs through immanence and its excess.

The thieves in *Inside Man* leave no trace of their theft. They don't take any money from the bank or anything registered in any of the safe-deposit boxes. When the police storm the bank, all that they find are hostages and no criminals. The thieves organize the robbery so that everything remains as it was within the bank, and yet they manage to steal diamonds worth millions of dollars. They accomplish this because of their awareness of the excess that exists within the bank and their ability to create a site of internal excess where the leader of the gang, Dalton Russell, can hide for a week.

The diamonds that the thieves steal come from a safe-deposit box that apparently doesn't exist according to the bank's records. When Detectives Keith Frazier and Bill Mitchell (Chiwetel Ejiofor) search for the contents of all the boxes, they find one number missing on the ledger that they examine. The missing signifier on the list of safe-deposit boxes indicates an excess among them: it is the number of the box that contains the diamonds that the bank founder Arthur Case obtained during his dealings with the Nazis as they deported Jews to death camps. These diamonds are part of the illicitly obtained wealth that enabled Case to found the bank, but they cannot exist as part of the official bank records. Case keeps the diamonds and a record of his agreement with the Nazis, though he hides them amid hundreds of other safe-deposit boxes.

When the thieves escape, they do so in two forms, both of which suggest their commitment to immanence rather than transcendence. The leader of the thieves, Dalton Russell, hides inside the bank itself in a room that the thieves create for him during the robbery. A week after the robbery, Russell breaks through the wall he had hidden behind, climbs into a storage room, and simply walks out of the bank with the diamonds. He can hide inside the bank because there is an excess within, just as Case's private box functions as an immanent excess.

The other members of his gang hide among the hostages when the police raid the bank. Because they dress the hostages alike and interchange themselves among them during the robbery, none of the hostages can identify any of the thieves. The thieves appear as part of the group of hostages. Here again, Lee shows an excess that haunts an immanent field. The group of hostages can provide a hiding place for the thieves insofar as it exceeds itself. Any attempt at transcendence would become apparent to the police, but they cannot see the excess of immanence that immanence itself conceals.

The significance of Lee's manipulation of time in *Inside Man* is also linked to the relationship between immanence and transcendence. In almost every heist film, the heist occurs within the filmic discourse before the investigation of the heist. This order adheres to a standard chronology. But Lee's film includes Detective Frazier and Mitchell's interviews of the hostages (and unknown perpetrators), which take place in diegetic time after the robbery, during the time of the robbery. Lee cuts from the negotiations between the detectives and Russell while the robbery is going on to the interviews with the hostages that take place after the police have stormed the bank.

This formal decision reflects Lee's constant preoccupation with showing the absence of any outside to a situation. What happens after the end of the robbery is already implicitly included within the robbery itself as an excess that cannot be accounted for. By showing the interviews interspersed within the robbery, Lee makes evident through the form of the film the excess of immanence that manifests itself also in the content. Even though *Inside Man* is not one of Lee's more politically themed films, it nonetheless provides one of the clearest examples of his vision of how political change must transpire. Change occurs not through transcendence or escape but through going further inside the social structure to identify with its excess.

Clockers appears to violate Lee's insistence on the absence of any outside. The film ends in a traditional Hollywood fashion: Detective Rocco Klein places the reformed drug dealer Strike on a train so that he can escape the violence of his New York neighborhood. But this escape does not involve an outside. Strike's devotion to the train defines him as a character, and when he boards the train out of town at the end of the film, he embraces his own singularity rather than retreating to an external site. Strike escapes the trap of his New York neighborhood through what exists within that neighborhood but doesn't belong to it—his excessive devotion to the train. Even at the points where Lee's films seem to depict the possibility of transcendence, they emphasize that this transcendence remains immanent.

The absence of any transcendent realm is most evident in the narrative structure of *Girl 6*. The film begins with Girl 6 auditioning for a part in a film with Quentin Tarantino (played by himself). The audition begins with a monologue in which Girl 6 directly addresses the camera. After she speaks barely more than a sentence, Tarantino interrupts her and upbraids her for her failure to perform properly. When she tries to explain herself, he insists, "Don't talk, listen." But this rudeness, which we might expect from a famous director, acts as a prelude to his subsequent demand that she take off her shirt and expose her breasts. Because the role calls for nudity, Tarantino wants to see Girl 6 naked. It's clear that obtaining the role depends more on the physical appearance of Girl 6 than her acting ability, which is why Tarantino evinces no interest in the monologue and requires her to remove her shirt.

Though she feels uncomfortable and initially demurs, Girl 6 does acquiesce and reveal her breasts. As she does so, Lee cuts to a slightly grainier shot that mimics the filming of the audition, so that we become aware that we are seeing Girl 6 at this point through the camera. She is here in a fantasy world that the director creates. But after halfway removing her shirt, Girl 6 pulls it back up and decides to leave the audition. The humiliation of the nudity outweighs for her the possibility of the role. This leads to her career as a phone-sex operator, where she feels much more comfortable with the fantasy space.

What's important about this opening scene is not simply the condemnation of Hollywood's treatment of women and their objectification but rather the closed world that it suggests. As the film presents it, Girl 6 has no opportunities for money making other than the use of her sexuality, and phone sex represents a more attractive option than acting in Hollywood, at least based on this initial scene. After trying to make money distributing flyers for computer training, Girl 6 turns to phone sex, and this enables her to earn money while delving into a fantasy world that she plays a part in creating, in contrast to the Hollywood audition. But even this turn to phone sex leaves her within the same world that she tries to leave when she departs from the audition. She gains her living through men who use her as an object for the fulfillment of their sexual fantasies.

At the end of the film, Girl 6 earns enough money from phone sex to move to Los Angeles and try again to enter the film industry. She has an audition similar to the one that opens the film, this time with another director (Ron Silver), who seems more understanding than Tarantino. The new director allows Girl 6 to finish her monologue and seems more interested in how she acts and what she has to say. But in the end, he repeats Tarantino's demand: the film calls for nudity, and she must be willing to take off her shirt in the audition. In this penultimate scene of the film, however, Girl 6 does not first begin to remove her shirt and then leave. She refuses directly and walks out of the audition.

By creating a parallel between the opening and closing of the film, Lee reveals that there is no space of transcendence. Going to Los Angeles does not change the unacceptable demands of the film industry that were present in New York. Even if one director seems kinder, the endgame remains the same. But what does change is the attitude that Girl 6 herself takes toward the director's demand. While she partially gives in and then breaks down in the film's first scene, at the end she just walks out without any emotional response. Her investment in her excessive singularity enables her to transcend a situation that has no space for transcendence. At the conclusion of the film, she remains in its confined world, but she exceeds that world.

As Girl 6 walks out of the audition, Lee highlights the immanence of the filmic world in a more pronounced way than in any of his other films. She walks out over the star of Dorothy Dandridge on Hollywood Boulevard, and the film cuts to a long shot of her crossing the street and walking toward a cinema. On the marquee for Mann's Chinese Theater on the other side of the street is the film *Girl 6*, which suggests that she remains within the filmic world even if she goes to the movies within that world. The final sense of the complete immanence of the filmic world occurs through how the film announces its ending. On a billboard in the top left of the image, we see "The End" written. In almost every film that announces its end, "The End" occurs extradiegetically, either over the last scene or after it. But here Lee includes this announcement within the filmic diegesis. He does this to underline the absence of any transcendent space. There is nowhere outside of the diegesis to which the spectator or Girl 6 herself might retreat. The only possibility for transcendence lies within the excesses of immanence, such as that of Girl 6 herself.

The immanence of Lee's filmic universe reaches its apogee in *Red Hook Summer*, a film that includes references to several of Lee's earlier films. As Flik interacts with the Brooklyn neighborhood, characters from other films appear. We see Mookie (Spike Lee) from *Do the Right Thing*, still delivering pizza for Sal's Famous; Nola Darling from *She's Gotta Have It*, who has become Mother Darling (Tracy Camilla Johns) and a Jehovah's Witness; and Detective Flood (Isaiah Whitlock, Jr.) from *She Hate Me* and *25th Hour*, who gives his characteristic line, the elongated "shit." These intertextual references are not merely Lee's attempt to please the longtime viewers of his films with allusions that only they will understand. Instead, they testify to the field of immanence that Lee develops in his filmic universe. One cannot escape to the outside, even when one leaves one film and enters another. Escape is possible, but it requires remaining within the immanent world that confronts us. In Lee's filmic worlds, there is no space outside into which one might escape, but one can nonetheless escape through internal excess. The problem with the idea of an outside or a transcendent beyond is that it leads directly to paranoia, the idea that someone else has a monopoly on this outside. By locating excess in an internal site, Lee attempts to fight against the logic of paranoia, even when paranoia is not his explicit target.

Disturbing the Spectator

Though Spike Lee has never made a film in 3D, he nonetheless aims at creating a sense in the spectator that the events on the screen are coming at them. The depictions of passion that he creates disrupt any position of stable spectatorship. When spectators watch a Lee film, they witness their investment in paranoia and their complicity in racist structures of thought. One enjoys a Spike Lee film, but one enjoys it too much. The films force spectators to avow an excessive passion that becomes disturbing when it is avowed.

Even when Lee's films present characters with whom spectators can identify, the films encourage spectators to identify with what is disturbing and excessive about them. Identification, which typically serves a stabilizing function for spectators, becomes destabilizing and revolutionary. In this sense, Lee's films do not offer the pleasures that we expect when we go to the movies. Instead, they provide a disturbing enjoyment that spectators must suffer. This constitutes the appeal of his films and, at the same time, the reason why they receive such virulent attacks—and perhaps why none has received an Academy Award nomination for Best Picture. The disturbance of the spectator's equilibrium becomes clearest when Lee resorts to a filmic device developed in the very origins of the cinema.

One of the aspects of early silent cinema that disappears with the development of classical form is direct address to the camera. Classical form creates the impression of a closed cinema world that the spectators observe as if they are looking through a keyhole. This differentiates cinema from its most proximate art form, the theater. As Christian Metz recounts in *The Imaginary Signifier,* "Cinematic voyeurism, *unauthorised* scopophilia, is from the outset more strongly established than that of the theatre in direct line from the primal scene. Certain precise features of the institution contribute to this affinity: the obscurity surrounding the onlooker, the aperture of the screen with its inevitable keyhole effect" (63). Metz's statement doesn't consider early films that often employ direct address and thus resemble the theater or the vaudeville show, films like those of Georges Méliès or even a more narratively inclined filmmaker like Edwin Porter. Direct address that defies the keyhole effect remains part of the cinematic aesthetic after the turn away, by 1908, from what Tom Gunning calls the "cinema of attractions." For example, D. W. Griffith's *Birth of a Nation* uses direct address on multiple occasions through its intertitles and through the famous close-up of John Wilkes Booth (Raoul Walsh) just before he assassinates Lincoln (Joseph Henebary). But by the end of the silent era and throughout the classical sound era, direct address almost completely disappears from the cinema. When it occurs in more recent films, like *Ferris Bueller's Day Off* (John Hughes, 1986), it consists almost entirely in a character narrating or explaining events to the camera and has the effect of helping to establish the self-contained filmic space rather than calling it into question.

In contrast to Hughes's use of direct address to keep the spectator at a proper distance and yet assist in identifying with the filmic space as self-contained, Spike Lee deploys direct address in the fashion of the early masters of silent cinema. In fact, his use of direct address to the camera in films like *Do the Right Thing* and *25th Hour* recalls the famous image of the thief firing his gun at the spectator in the concluding shot of *The Great Train Robbery* (Edwin S. Porter, 1903). After the narrative sequence of the film ends, Porter adds this completely excessive scene of direct address that violates the keyhole effect established through the rest of the film's running time. Rather than shooting the spectator, however, Lee's characters who address the camera directly do something far worse: they typically spew racial or other types of epithets and display great enjoyment in doing so.

A director might, of course, simply depict characters using offensive language during the course of the narrative, and this could serve as an indictment of the characters and their mindsets. But the depiction of racist or sexist or homophobic language has two major failings that direct address attempts to correct. When we see characters saying offensive terms, we remain at a distance from them and feel insulated from what is being said; the keyhole effect enables spectators to keep their psychical as well as physical distance. But even more importantly, the enjoyment that underlies the offensive terms cannot easily manifest itself within the confines of the cinema's narrative structure. Direct address corrects these two problems.

When we see the characters in *Do the Right Thing* launch into stereotypical diatribes while speaking directly to the camera, we as spectators become the addressees of these comments, and we see how much the characters enjoy the aggression inherent in their language. As Ed Guerrero explains, "On the block in the harsh light of this hottest day of the year, a series of working-class men of different races, ethnicities and groups emphatically address the camera and vent their stored anger at a designated racial *other*" (52–53). Though Guerrero is correct to note that the characters express their rage toward racial others, it is important to add that they direct this rage not only toward the camera but also toward the spectator. As a viewer of *Do the Right Thing*, one endures multiple assaults in the form of ethnic slurs.

The series of shots in direct address begins with Mookie's response to Pino's racism. He says, "Dago, wop, garlic-breath, guinea, pizza-slinging, spaghetti-bending, Vic Damone, Perry Como, Luciano Pavarotti, Sole Mio, non-singing motherfucker." The film cuts immediately from Mookie's direct address to Pino's. Pino replies, "You gold-teeth, gold-chain-wearing, fried-chicken-and-biscuit-eating, monkey, ape, baboon, big thigh, fast running, three-hundred-sixty-degree-basketball-dunking, spade, moulinyan. Take your fucking piece of pizza and go the fuck back to Africa." The next shot depicts a minor character, Stevie (Luis Ramos), articulating his anti-Korean racism. He proclaims, "You slant-eyed, me-no-speak-American, own every fruit and vegetable stand in New York, Reverend Moon, Summer Olympics '88, Korean kick-boxing bastard." Lee adds two more diatribes in direct address, one from a police officer attacking Puerto Ricans, denouncing the Puerto Rican as a "fifteen-in-a-car, thirty-in-an-apartment . . . cocksucker," and another from the Korean grocer attacking Jews, characterizing the Jew as a "bagel and lox,

B'nai B'rith asshole." These instances of direct cinematic address remove us from the conventions of narrative cinema and return us to cinema's origins, a time in which spectacle and enjoyment took precedence over the pleasures of narrative continuity.

The disruption of the spectator's formal expectations evinces an irruption of a passion that exceeds the diegesis, and Lee registers this passion through the return to direct address. The critic Elizabeth Hope Finnegan makes this point in her analysis of the film. She notes, "By removing this sequence from the diegesis (the story world), we are not given an opportunity to become involved narratively with any potential motivations, intentions, or justifications for the words. The words are simply there—inescapable, commanding out attention, simultaneously making us the object of these words and condemning us as potential speakers of them" (87). Direct address produces a disruptiveness that could not occur within the indirect form of a narrative structure. The slurs appear out of context and in the form of a verbal assault, spoken in aggressive tones.

What stands out in this sequence of direct address is what the characters are able to say. Though people today still employ these derogatory terms and stereotypes, they simply cannot be uttered in polite society. No one can go on a job interview, for instance, and refer to an Italian American as a "wop" or an African American as a "spade." None of these racist slurs are acceptable in public discourse—which is why they remain enjoyable to utter—and yet they continue to play a predominant role in private conversations and thoughts. That is to say, the excesses of racism are today largely confined to a fantasy space, which allows them to manifest themselves through informing how people act without being publicly articulated. The genius of this sequence in *Do the Right Thing* is that it brings the excessive enjoyment of the racist fantasies to light and assails the spectator with the obscenity of this racism. As the characters directly address the camera, it is apparent that they enjoy what they say, and this passion actually motivates them to mouth the racist stereotypes. These stereotypes have a hold on us because we enjoy them, and Lee's film demands that the spectator experience and confront this passion for the stereotype.

Though direct address in Lee's films often disturbs the spectator through the display of the character's obscene passion for aggressive stereotypes, it also has the effect, like Lee's signature dolly shot, of removing the character from the filmic world. The character speaking to the camera exists outside of the diegetic space. In the opening of *Inside Man*, Lee uses this alienation to great effect as it obscures Dalton Russell's location and thus makes possible the twist toward the end of the film, when it becomes evident that he is hiding in a small cell within the bank itself. As Lori Harrison-Kahan points out in her essay "Inside *Inside Man*," "While the secret of Russell's location is one of the film's suspenseful twists, it is further significant that the opening refuses our knowledge of his location—a decontextualization of place that is repeated throughout the film" (49). Direct address disorients the spectator by showing the irreducibility of the character to its place. Dalton Russell appears to speak from a prison cell, but we learn later that it is a cell of his own making that enables him actually to avoid prison. If we think of him in terms of his environment, we fall into a fundamental deception that the form of direct address leads us to avoid. Direct address enacts a decontextualization that reveals how subjectivity exceeds its place.

The disturbance created by Monty's use of direct address in *25th Hour* goes beyond that in *Do the Right Thing* or *Inside Man*. This is primarily due to the form that Monty's speech takes on. Rather than seeing Monty himself speak, we see him looking in the mirror, and the mirror reflection directly addresses the camera. Monty sees "Fuck you!" written in pen at the bottom of the bathroom mirror of a bar, and this leads his mirror image to articulate a litany of people he wants to brand with this insult, while Monty himself says nothing. His mirror image assails many groups, and among them, he includes "the Korean grocers," "the Enron assholes," and "the corrupt cops." Even Christ becomes a target, as he says, "Fuck J.C. He got off easy." During each moment of the diatribe, Lee provides a visual representation of Monty's target, which we don't see in *Do the Right Thing*. When he says "Fuck the uptown brothers" for their style of basketball play, we see black basketball players commit the very offenses that he enumerates (failing to pass, traveling with the ball). Monty's direct address is longer and more detailed than any that occurs in *Do the Right Thing*, but because it comes from his mirror image, it forces the spectator to evaluate it differently.

Monty's direct address
to the mirror in *25th Hour.*

By having Monty's mirror image speak directly to the camera, Lee makes it even clearer than in *Do the Right Thing* that the subject speaking here exceeds Monty himself. The distance between this excess and Monty becomes clear immediately after the monologue concludes. Lee cuts to a reverse shot from the perspective of the mirror that shows Monty himself, and he says, "No, fuck you, Montgomery Brogan. You had it all, and you threw it away, you dumb fuck." Here, Monty recognizes that he himself embodies the excess that he wants to eliminate. It is a recognition that the other characters who directly address the camera and reveal their excess do not come to, and it indicates the privileged use of this form in *25th Hour.*

The use of direct address in *Crooklyn,* in contrast to *Do the Right Thing* and *25th Hour,* does not seem to mark a point of disturbance for the spectator. Instead of reciting offensive stereotypes directly into the camera, Carolyn Carmichael speaks to her daughter Troy through direct address to the camera at the end of the film. Though Carolyn offers reassurance to Troy, the form of this reassurance nonetheless creates a disturbance in the manner of the other instances of direct address in Lee's films. Lee shoots the sequences of direct address after Carolyn dies, and as a result, we see a dead person speaking directly to us. After Carolyn becomes sick with cancer, she disappears entirely from the film: her suffering and death is present only through its absence from the narrative. This absence transforms the reassurance of her posthumous direct address into a disturbing spectral appearance in the film. The form of her appearance supersedes the succor of its content. But *Crooklyn* also reveals how Lee's ability to disturb the spectator through the form of his films extends far beyond the use of direct address.

Ironically, Spike Lee's most disturbing film is one of the two films that he made—the other is *Malcolm X*—that did not earn an R rating. The PG-13 *Crooklyn* uses an anamorphic lens to distort the image when the main character Troy goes for an extended stay with relatives in Virginia. The film depicts the Carmichael family driving south from Brooklyn with a standard lens, but from the moment that they enter the house of Troy's Uncle Clem and Aunt Song, the image becomes visibly distorted. Due to the use of the anamorphic lens during filming and not during projection, the characters appear much narrower than they would ordinarily look. The effect of this sequence disturbed many reviewers and critics of the film, and it also led theaters to put up signs warning viewers that this distortion in the middle of the film did not indicate a problem with the projection.

Though some critics celebrated Lee's inventiveness, others took him to task for the indulgence that the anamorphic lens suggests. For instance, Tom Stempel finds *Crooklyn* "an otherwise charming coming-of-age story," but the sequence in Virginia ruins the film for him. He complains, "Theatres . . . already printed signs to put outside the auditoriums telling the audience the effect was intended. Audiences were still baffled and upset by the distortion" (151). Stempel takes it as axiomatic that an effect that leaves the audience "baffled and upset" is necessarily a failure. But this is integral to Lee's filmic project. The audience's enjoyment of a film, in contrast to the pleasure found in it, is inextricable from being "baffled and upset." Enjoyment takes us beyond the boundaries that establish our identity, and thus it necessarily entails some suffering, like the suffering that the audiences for *Crooklyn* experience.

With the anamorphic lens, Lee doesn't simply disrupt the spectator's expectations for the sake of doing so. Instead, he aims at forcing spectators to reconceive their idea of normalcy. Troy travels from a raucous house in Brooklyn to a suburban domestic space in Virginia. Uncle Clem, Aunt Song, and their daughter Viola appear to live out the American Dream. While the Brooklyn household and neighborhood is saturated with conflict, the Virginia household and neighborhood is completely peaceful. Lee never depicts any trouble arising, except for what Troy's resistance to the harmonious situation creates. But the anamorphic lens calls this harmonious situation into question.

The film does not so much denigrate the relatives from the South as it casts doubt on the apparent harmony of the suburban middle-class lifestyle. For bell hooks, this is a limitation of the film and of Lee's vision as a filmmaker. The disturbing effect of the anamorphic lens marks its failure as a filmic device. In *Reel to Real,* she says, "The switch to an anamorphic lens confuses. No doubt that is why signs were placed at ticket booths telling viewers that this change did not indicate a problem with the projector. Fancy attempts at cover-up aside, in these scenes Lee mockingly caricatures in an uninteresting fashion the southern black middle class" (39). As hooks sees it, the distortion functions purely as mockery, and certainly Aunt Song is the victim of critique in the film, especially when she removes Troy's braids and straightens her hair. But the more significant point of the anamorphic lens lies in its commentary on the status of the normal life that the Virginia relatives seem to have.

Lee turns to the anamorphic lens to emphasize that normalcy itself is a distortion. One constitutes a normal situation through some form of distortion that makes this situation possible, a distortion captured by the anamorphic lens. In daily existence, normalcy obscures this distortion through its constancy. The idea of what is normal bombards us from second to second so that we can't see the specific restrictions that enable it to function. These restrictions become visible in the content of Troy's experience at her relatives' house, but even more so in the film's form. If one properly watches this film, one can no longer think about the American norm without at the same time thinking about the distortion that founds it.

The distortion that occurs in *Bamboozled* is less formal than that in *Crooklyn* but more fundamental. The film bombards the spectator from beginning to end with an excessive dose of racism in America, so much so that some critics accused the film of exaggerating its depiction to such an extent that this attack on American racism loses its sting. The film presents vulgar racist stereotypes, characters performing in blackface, overtly racist language, and a barrage of negative black images from film and television history. The basic idea of the film—that a television network would air a show with black characters in blackface set in a watermelon patch—appears impossible to believe. Yet the film's excess is the key to its efficacy. Because it never relents from its onslaught of racist imagery and language, *Bamboozled* has the effect of normalizing the excess or enabling us to see that what passes for our normal everyday reality is actually underwritten by a surfeit of racism that largely remains invisible, at least to those who aren't looking for it.

Racism continues to thrive because it hides its excessiveness and manifests itself through subtleties. No network would air *Mantan: The New Millennium Minstrel Show.* But a major network does air *COPS,* a show that traffics in the stereotype of black criminality, and Hollywood does produce films like *Tower Heist* (Brett Ratner, 2011), which uses the black criminal's incompetence as a source for comedy. No network executive would contend that his black wife and biracial children give him the right to use the word "nigger," as Dunwitty does in Lee's film, but Quentin Tarantino has defended the use of this word in *Pulp Fiction* (1994) by invoking his upbringing among black people. No black actor would give his Emmy Award to the white presenter he doesn't really know and misidentifies, like Pierre does with Matthew Modine in *Bamboozled,* but Ving Rhames did give his Golden Globe Award to fellow nominee Jack Lemmon. In these instances and many others, *Bamboozled* creates an extreme situation out of events that actually occur without much fanfare. No one protests *COPS* or *Tower Heist,* and though Lee and a few others objected to *Pulp Fiction,* there was little public outcry against the film. By making these everyday occurrences excessive, Lee's film forces the spectator to reevaluate the status of what is acceptable.

For the spectator of *Bamboozled,* there is no place safe from the onslaught of excess. It occurs most prominently through the television program that features characters in blackface, a setting in a watermelon patch, a musical group known as the Alabama Porch Monkeys, and an emcee whose tagline is "Niggers is a beautiful thing." At every turn, there is much more overt racism than spectators typically see. The excess permeates throughout the film, from those involved with the program to those militantly opposed to it.

The creator of *Mantan,* Pierre Delacroix, is Harvard-educated and successful in the entertainment industry. But his affected accent reveals that he tries too hard to fit into the white world; his accent appears to derive more from an attempt to avoid sounding "black" than from any effort to associate himself with a particular region (and the accent is not easily identifiable with a place). The spectator hears Pierre's voiceover throughout the film, which serves as a constant reminder of the false accent. Pierre's conformity has a parallel in the black militancy of the Mau-Maus, a musical and political group headed by Julius (Mos Def), the brother of Pierre's assistant Sloan.

When Julius first appears in the film, greeting Sloan at her apartment, he tells her that he has abandoned his slave name Julius in favor of "Big Blak Afrika." When Sloan asks Big Blak Afrika what he and his group are revolting against, he can't answer. And later we see the group decide to title their new album *Blak Is Blak* without the "c" as another sign of nonsensical revolt. They correctly view the white power structure as oppressive, but they cannot even concretely identify this structure, let alone conceive of an alternative to it. All they do is play with signifiers—changing a name, asserting a tautological identity—and this mirrors the excessive conformity of Pierre. He changes his name from "Peerless" to "Pierre" and affects an accent in order to fit in, while the Mau-Maus revolt only on the level of the signifier. This becomes further evident when they plan to act: they repeat after each other multiple times, "You know what I mean?" and "You know what I'm saying?" But they say nothing to which these rhetorical questions might correspond. Their revolt goes too far and results in numerous deaths because it doesn't go far enough. Their radical break from the prevailing signification marks a failure to break from the structure that undergirds that signification.

The portrait of the Mau-Maus is perhaps the most disturbing aspect of *Bamboozled*. Lee names them for the Mau-Maus of Kenya, a revolutionary group that fought for freedom from political oppression. But they are similar to this group in name only. As Tracey Owens Patton and Deborah McGriff note, "The *Bamboozled* Mau-Maus merely focused on the militancy of the Kenyan Mau-Maus while failing to reveal underlying issues of economic and political self-sufficiency. In their failure to comprehend the multiple dimensions of revolutionary rhetoric they become caricatures of the Kenyan Mau-Maus" (93). Though the Mau-Maus in the film mimic the revolt of their Kenyan namesakes, they do so only on the level of the signifier.

The Mau-Maus are the primary force that we see reacting against the racism of the television show and the society, but their reaction produces nothing but increased brutality when it results in the death of Manray and their own deaths at the hands of the police. Their shared name and political distance from the Kenyan Mau-Maus underscores the lack of any revolutionary alternative within the filmic world. The spectator has no position outside the various excesses with which to identify. Even Sloan, who appears as a force of moral righteousness throughout the film, plays a role in the creation of the show and stays in her job after its success, despite her objections to its trajectory. And her final act of killing Pierre appears as much an attempt to expunge her own guilt as to render justice.

One cannot watch *Bamboozled* without finding oneself implicated in its racist excesses. In this way, it shows that the excess of racism so infiltrates our social structures that there is no escape from it. The white characters who try to enter black identity, like Dunwitty, cannot escape the excess any more than those who try to maintain an attitude of color-blindness, like the white writers for the show. But the black characters become caught in the same trap: they either capitulate to racism or blindly strike out like the Mau-Maus. The protestors outside the network offices, like Al Sharpton and Johnnie Cochran (playing themselves), play only a miniscule part in the film. In the world of *Bamboozled,* the type of excess embodied by Malcolm X appears only as a marker for what isn't there. As Pierre points out to the white writers, "To ask Denzel to wear blackface would be foolish." As he says this, the film shows Washington playing Malcolm X and telling a crowd that they have been "bamboozled." By leaving such a figure present only as an absence, Lee offers the spectator no respite. As Phil Chidester and Jamel Santa Cruze Bell put it in their analysis of the film as a new form of satire, "In the end, viewers are denied in *Bamboozled* an opportunity in the classical satirical sense to openly identify with the work's author by joining in a concerted attack against a single, more powerful target" (211). One must endure the montage of racist black collectibles and the constant presence of blackface without a clear alternative.

One cannot even withdraw from the field of possibilities that the film presents. Just as Lee uses a sublime shot of the Klan in the moonlight in *Malcolm X, Bamboozled* prompts the spectator to find enjoyment in the performance of the show. Lee includes moments of genuine comedy, such as the sketch in which Mantan and Sleep 'n Eat constantly interrupt each other while nonetheless correctly anticipating what the other is about to say. This sketch occurs with the characters in blackface and amid the plantation setting, which work to tug the spectator in opposed directions. The film encourages one to see the humor and even laugh, but at the same time, one cannot forget the object of one's laughter. In this way, spectators find themselves implicated in the excess that they see. To refuse to laugh and to maintain a position above the filmic world is to insist on a false innocence that the film doesn't permit. The proper spectator enjoys and recognizes the trauma attached to this enjoyment.

Bamboozled is Lee's most disturbing film and his greatest success because it never leaves the terrain of excess—with its intense and constant concern with racist imagery—and yet it creates a sense of everyday reality out of its excesses. The film lays bare the excess that inheres in our social reality not only by exaggerating the racism of contemporary television but also by placing the racist images that proliferate in the society in juxtaposition with each other. The film's many montage sequences—including the final one, which serves as a condemnation of the history of Hollywood—prohibit us from seeing racism as an isolated exception or as an individual problem, which are the common modes of avoiding the confrontation with it. The structural nature of our racist excess becomes apparent through the film's unrelenting editing.

Lee's use of montage in *Bamboozled* and in other films like *When the Levees Broke* piles up images to create a sense of the social totality. By using montage in this way, Lee identifies himself as a partisan of dialectics as Georg Lukács defines the concept. In *History and Class Consciousness,* Lukács identifies dialectics with a capacity to envision the social totality from apparently isolated particulars. He states, "The essence of the dialectical method lies in the fact that in every aspect correctly grasped by the dialectic the whole totality is comprehended and that the whole method can be unravelled from every single aspect" (170). Despite his opposition to modernist techniques like montage, Lukács here provides a concise account of what montage accomplishes. By grouping together a series of single images, it provides a sense of the "whole totality" that would otherwise remain unrecognizable. Through his use of montage, Lee creates a dialectics of excess. He multiplies the images and lays bare the totality that their apparent isolation obscures.

In *Bamboozled,* the montage sequences focus on performers putting on blackface, stereotypical collectibles like the "Jolly Nigger Bank," and, most significantly, the scenes from film and television history. Near the conclusion of act 2 of the four-act *When the Levees Broke,* Lee includes a montage of dead bodies left in the water in New Orleans. This montage occurs after the film provides a political context for the natural disaster and thus shows the result of the utter neglect of the people of New Orleans. Likewise, at the end of act 3, Lee's film uses the montage of multiple bodies and concludes this part with an individual woman whose child was among the dead. Through these parallel conclusions, the film links the "whole totality" with the "single aspect." We can only glimpse this totality through a filmic effect that piles up the bodies in a way that reality itself does not.

When the Levees Broke does not only reveal excess when it employs montage; it is also apparent in the political response to the catastrophe. Lee's film is not about a natural disaster but about how a political crisis created a natural disaster. The lack of preparation and the lack of response to the hurricane weigh far more than the natural act itself, which has almost no role at all in *When the Levees Broke.* In addition to highlighting the devastation suffered by the residents of New Orleans and Mississippi, Lee includes the excesses of political leaders and the excessive responses to them. He shows President Bush's famous praise of FEMA head Michael Brown (a figure somewhat redeemed in the sequel, *If God Is Willing and da Creek Don't Rise*). Bush says to Brown, "And Brownie, you're doing a heck of a job." Given the colossal failure of FEMA, Lee repeats this scene three times to register the incredible irony formally. Later, we see a man from Mississippi approach Vice President Cheney, who was visiting the disaster site, and twice yell at him, "Go fuck yourself, Mr. Cheney." The inclusion of this act reveals excess as the only proper response to the crime committed against the impoverished people of the region. In addition, the film depicts a variety of signs and statements attacking the political leadership at the time. Lee includes these excesses of the power structure and these excessive responses to the power to underline the political stakes of the supposed natural disaster. Through these excesses, we can see the social totality that created the catastrophe. Lee's dialectical approach occurs in the formal choices that he makes.

Lee's approach is dialectical not only through its insistence on approaching the whole totality through excess but also through the path that it takes to arrive at that totality. We tend to think of the totality as the product of an objective look, a look that rises above or even puts together all particular perspectives. But Lee arrives at the totality through an excess of perspective. We only grasp the totality if we look askew rather than attempting to gain a neutral look. Here again, Lee remains faithful to the insights of Georg Lukács, who posits the slanted perspective of the proletariat as the only one capable of gaining insight into social relations in their totality. The attempt to remain neutral has the effect of blinding one to the role that excess plays in social relations, while an engaged perspective enables one to see excess constantly manifesting itself and distorting how individuals relate to each other within the social structure.

The distortion of the look proliferates throughout *Bamboozled*. In almost every scene of the film, Lee includes a variety of low- and high-angle shots that disturb the spectator's expectations. The film rarely permits us to look in an apparently neutral fashion. This is a point made by Rachael Ziady Delue in her interpretation of the film's handling of race. She notes, "Lee positions the camera so that his scenes are not always windows onto the world, as if seen by the naked eye from an embodied point of view within a linear-perspective scheme; rather, the world of *Bamboozled* is askew, seen from above or below or from around the corner, under the table, or way, way, way down the hall" (69). These ubiquitous distortions in the film have the effect of forcing the spectator to become aware of perspective, not to dismiss what appears in the image but to recognize how engagement makes this recognition possible. Without the excess of Lee's filmic distortion, one would remain blind to the social world that the film presents and be left instead with a series of isolated instances of racism. Only the engaged perspective sees the totality.

Lee even brings this sense of a necessary engagement to his documentary filmmaking. Though his documentaries have fewer of the formal flourishes than the fiction films, the idea of an excessive engagement remains. There is no such thing as a straightforward Spike Lee film. Even the documentaries that concern themselves with bringing historical and contemporary injustices to light turn to formal eccentricities that one rarely finds in documentary filmmaking. For instance, in his follow-up film about the catastrophe in New Orleans, *If God Is Willing and da Creek Don't Rise,* Lee shoots the talking heads that typically appear in documentaries in an atypical way. Though we often initially see people speak in a standard shot, facing the camera, Lee usually cuts to a side angle that shows the speaker in profile. There is no ostensible reason for the cut to this angle, but it has the effect of accentuating the emphasis on the disruptiveness of film form itself.

The constant cuts from a head-on shot to a profile shot is a subtle allusion to Jean-Luc Godard's *Deux ou trois choses que je sais d'elle* (*Two or Three Things That I Know about Her,* 1968), in which the film's voiceover narration reflects on which image is the true one—the head-on shot or the one in profile—during the film's famous café scene. But Lee uses this form to a different end than Godard. Godard's aim is to draw attention to cinematic production and manipulation, whereas Lee wants to demonstrate how the distorted shot leads us to insight into the totality that would otherwise escape us. Lee's documentaries about New Orleans rely on a particular perspective to create a sense of the totality of the situation that would otherwise be lost. He uses the catastrophe as a meditation on class and racial inequities in the nation, and at every point he connects the natural disaster to a moral and political one. It requires an engaged perspective to make these connections, and this is what the profile shots in *If God Is Willing* make clear.

Lee is a disturbing filmmaker not because of the uncomfortable content of his films but because he produces a form that ensconces the spectator in the excesses of society without any clear way out. The insights of his films always come with the traumatic recognition that we are complicit in what we see. Even in his documentaries, Lee refuses the spectator any neutral position outside the subject matter. Film enables us to see in ways that we cannot ordinarily see, and Lee will constantly make use of this quality to disturb our ingrained perspectives.

The Effect of Spike Lee

Critics often talk about Spike Lee's importance in paving the way for other African American directors like John Singleton and Carl Franklin, and with his production company 40 Acres and a Mule, Lee has created many opportunities for aspiring black filmmakers. But Lee does not create a path that others can follow. His films are always idiosyncratic, and his formal style does not invite imitation. His use of formal devices like the anamorphic lens in *Crooklyn* could not become a mainstream filmic technique. Instead, these devices allow him to stand out as a director. In fact, even for Lee himself, this technique is a hapax, a technique that a filmmaker could use only once. He develops his own film form that gives him a singularity. Often, critics find his films excessive, but it is precisely this excess that defines a Spike Lee film and attests to his lasting importance.

Though there have been numerous other filmmakers of excess throughout the history of cinema, perhaps none has explored the multiple manifestations that it takes on to the extent that Lee has. He begins by showing how excess defines us as subjects and enables us to enjoy our existence, and he moves to depictions of excess that reveal its role in racist outbursts of brutal violence. His films further show how excess develops through the power of fantasy or how it allows us to transcend the oppressiveness of our environment. Excess is at once what makes our lives worth living and what makes them unlivable. Lee never flinches from connecting the enjoyment that excess produces to its destructiveness. To access the one, we must come to grips with the other, and this is what his films ask us to do.

Despite the controversy that often overshadowed Lee's early films, the sheer number of outstanding films throughout his career finally established him as one of the great American directors, and with the appearance of so many critically acclaimed works, his filmography definitively took priority over his personality among reviewers. Though the ad hominem review was always a dubious approach to his films, his lasting achievement has made this response impossible. Even the most recalcitrant reviewers must now grapple with the films themselves and confront Lee's formal creativity.

Lee's status as a great American filmmaker has not, as one might expect, dulled his inventiveness. Though the number of American artists who were destroyed by early success is great, Lee has avoided this trap. Unlike Francis Ford Coppola, Arthur Penn, or even Martin Scorsese, one cannot identify a dropoff in Lee's filmmaking after his initial successes. Perhaps the closest parallel to Lee is Robert Altman, despite their difference in filmmaking style. Altman's films from the 1970s broke new ground in American cinema, but in the 1980s, he seemed to disappear until he reemerged with his two masterpieces, *The Player* (1992) and *Short Cuts* (1993). These films marked not only a return to the greatness of the films of the 1970s, like *McCabe and Mrs. Miller* (1971) or *The Long Goodbye* (1973), but their transcendence. A similar process occurs with Spike Lee.

Though Lee never had a filmmaking low point like *Popeye* (1980), the films of the 1990s did not achieve the impact of *Do the Right Thing,* and it seemed as if Lee had already made his one standout film. But *Summer of Sam* and *Bamboozled* in 1999 and 2000 represented his version of *The Player* and *Short Cuts.* From that moment on, his reputation was or should have been completely secure, but he also did not arrest his ability to discover new domains of excess. His turn to genre films and documentaries in the 2000s and 2010s did not stunt his formal creativity but rather provided new avenues for it to thrive. Though trademarks like the dolly tracking shot remain in a later film like *Inside Man,* new flourishes like the manipulation of cinematic time, which he uses to confound the identity of the criminal and the victim, begin to appear as well. With *Red Hook Summer,* he leads the spectator to believe that he's returning to the world

The singularity of Spike Lee. |

of an earlier film like *Do the Right Thing* or *Crooklyn*, only to introduce what might be the most disturbing turn in his entire cinematic career. The evolving aesthetic that Lee creates maintains his singularity while at the same time evincing a refusal to remain within a static identity. His filmmaking of excess constantly exceeds itself, and this movement demands that spectators keep watching. When we go to a Spike Lee film, we know that we will be confronted with excess, but we don't know the new form that this excess will take. His films force spectators to face their own excesses—their proclivities for racist paranoia or for suspicion of the other's enjoyment. But they also permit an enjoyment that one cannot find in most films. Even when Lee shows the most horrific images, he always does so in a way that privileges our enjoyment of them. No matter how opposed to the activities of the Klan we might be, we can't help but enjoy the shot of them riding toward the moon in *Malcolm X*. It is our capacity for passionate excesses that creates the possibility for overcoming all the situations that continue to oppress us.

Lee constructs a moral and political cinema, but this morality is inextricable from our capacity for passion. Morality, as Lee's cinema conceives it, doesn't involve the abandonment of an excessive passion but an embrace of it. Embracing our excessive passion is how we "do the right thing." The title of Lee's third feature acts as the defining statement of his cinematic career. But what stands out about this admonition is its complete absence of content. Neither *Do the Right Thing* nor any of Lee's other films explains exactly what the right thing is. He creates a moral cinema without any moral advice for the spectator.

The point of the films is not that the content of the "right thing" changes from situation to situation or from person to person. Instead, Lee's films show a total indifference to the content. Doing the right thing requires one to insist on one's excess and to inhabit the position of excessive singularity. This is the position embodied most clearly by Lee's signature dolly shot, which provides a succinct image of his morality. We must remain in our world but not of our world. We must imagine ourselves always in Lee's dolly shot, still within our environment and yet simultaneously transcending it.

Interview with Spike Lee |

A substantial portion of this interview first appeared on the Web site Hollywood.com, where the interviewer Lisa Collins worked as a senior editor and segment producer. An award-winning independent filmmaker, multimedia artist, and entertainment journalist, Collins's path intersects in many ways with that of Spike Lee, including the fact that both won a Student Academy Award. Collins earned her MFA in screenwriting and directing from Columbia University, and *Filmmaker* magazine named her "one of the 25 New Faces of Independent Film." In addition, her work has been presented in a retrospective at the Brooklyn Academy of Music by *Creatively Speaking*. As director/producer, Collins is currently in postproduction on *Oscar's Comeback* with her partner Mark Schwartzburt. *Oscar's Comeback* chronicles the worlds that collide behind the scenes at an annual festival in a small all-white town in rural South Dakota that champions their black native son, the pioneer filmmaker Oscar Micheaux. *Oscar's Comeback* has been awarded funding from a variety of sources. For further information or to donate to *Oscar's Comeback*, please visit www.oscarscomeback.com.

LISA COLLINS: Hectic Brooklyn in the '70s and '80s—there was an undeniable love/hate relationship between Italian Americans and black Americans. Can you speak a little to that?

SPIKE LEE: Well, here's the thing. Just growing up in Brooklyn, my experience . . . I've learned a lot because we're so similar, [as] so [many] people have been pointing out, and I've been acknowledging it.

LC: Many of your films investigate . . . deeply exposed roots—tensions and ties—connecting different ethnicities.

SL: Yeah, one could do a big article about it, if you look at the first two films I did, *Do the Right Thing* and *Jungle Fever*—and then there was *Summer of Sam*. They all dealt with the interaction of Italian Americans and African Americans.

LC: Coincidentally, I just bought a VHS copy of *Do the Right Thing* at a black-cinema video sale in Harlem. *Amazing* again!

SL: Wait, you still have a working VHS player? Damn.

LC: I know, I know—a little old school, it's true. Well, yeah, having watched it so recently, I wonder—how do you see *Do the Right Thing* playing [into these interconnections you've been highlighting]?

SL: You have to remember that I wrote *Do the Right Thing* right at the height of Howard Beach [the 1986 hate-crime murder of Michael Griffith in Queens]. That really prompted *Do the Right Thing*. At that time, New York City was racially polarized. I think Mayor Ed Koch had a lot to do with that. So, the idea was simple. I wanted to do a film on the hottest day of the summer that takes place on one block, and use this one block as a microcosm of the very strain at that moment. Is that [racial polarization] the case now? No, I think we've evolved. I think even with the Sean Bell case—I applaud how Mayor Bloomberg handled it . . . and African Americans were responsible with peaceful reactions. But also, Barack Obama wasn't possible back in 1989 either. I think that *Do the Right Thing* has really captured that [alarming] moment, and we've moved on. Thank God.

LC: So [in *Miracle at St. Anna*] you're charting part of that shift where blacks were more embraced back during World War II by European Italians, rather than by American Italians [in more recent decades]?

SL: You go to this film—now this is historical—[and] Italians for the most part in World War II loved the black soldiers. First of all, they were not really inundated with [American] racism and the prejudices and all that stuff. Also, they saw [the black soldiers] as liberators. They wanted to get out from under the tyranny of Mussolini, the fascists, and also the Nazis; and the majority of soldiers were black Americans. While we were shooting this film in Italy, several elderly Italians made the point to tell me how many fond memories they had of the black soldiers from World War II.

LC: When I was little, my old Polish-Jewish neighbor would often speak of being so thankful and relieved to see black servicemen [the first American rescuers she had laid eyes on] arrive at the concentration camp. Was there a World War II–specific tale you heard over there?

SL: True story: one lady who could speak a little bit of English told me how when she was an infant, she was dying, and her mother took her to the camp where the soldiers were staying. And the black doctors gave her the shots of penicillin, and she pulled through. Then she started crying because she was telling me this story and said, "I'm alive today because of the black soldiers that came to liberate our country." Realize, though, Italian Americans are different from Italians. The same way African Americans are different from Africans. There's that bond, the heritage, the blood [that they share], but a different socialization and a different way of life. Look at how people get along in this film versus *Do the Right Thing* or *Jungle Fever*.

LC: Simply put, the [*Miracle*] ensemble cast rules!

SL: Derek Luke, Michael Ealy, Laz Alonso, Omar Benson Miller—the credit goes to two people really: James McBride [*Miracle*'s scribe], first and foremost. James understood that these four people had to be very distinct, different aspects of African American men in 1944. I'd also like to thank my casting director Kim Coleman. She was great; we got the best people we could get. It really became a cohesive unit during the two-week boot camp prior. They all did wonderful performances.

LC: A lot of the reason that Barack Obama's campaign can exist as a reality today is because of the mediated messages that have helped prepare and remind "closed"/doubtful people across the board that, "Yes, hello, black Americans can lead and have positions of power too."

SL: Did you watch, um, *The State of the Union* by Chris Rock? What's it called again? No, it's, um, *Head of* . . .

LC and SL: *Head of State.* Yes!

SL: [shaking his head] There you go.

LC: Well, do you feel like you're, in part, a contributor of helping to put those images—particularly of black male leadership and strength—out there?

SL: That's not something I think about. Barack's in this position because of Dr. King, Malcolm [X], W. E. B. Du Bois, Booker T. Washington, Shirley Chisholm, JFK, Jesse Jackson, Al Sharpton, Harold Washington, David Dinkins, Carl B. Stokes—that's the stuff that has made Barack possible. Whether people want to hear it or not, this country has evolved. Racism and prejudice—not that it is eradicated, but the fact that our next president is . . . a man whose father was born in Uganda—ah, Kenya—this is huge! And it's [evolved] because of the American Patriots—these [legions of] black men that had fought in World War II, World War I, Vietnam, and Korea.

LC: Do you think *Miracle*'s particular "look" at World War II's atrocities helps give us a window into seeing how far people can take violence and cruelty past the edge of reason?

SL: I think an actor who plays that [executioner role] provides insight; but for me, I can't comprehend it actually. Yet there still comes a responsibility with that: the [1944 Nazi-led St. Anna] massacre that we shot in the film—we filmed it in the exact [historical] location where it took place. We were very respectful, and we shot that scene in two days. And you could feel the spirit and the souls of those men, women, and children [civilians] who were slaughtered. You could feel it. I'm not talking any "hocus pocus" stuff. That day, everybody felt their spirits and souls when we were shooting that scene. The hardest shot was that baby shot [the youngest victim, twenty days old]. That was a hard shot.

LC: Shifting gears, I must say, the film is lyrical. The young boy is perfectly cast. Village life is finely observed. A strong sensibility of the Italian neorealism film movement comes to life in *Miracle at St. Anna*, unlike multiple films that tried it but haven't quite gotten it. Is that film movement something you were/are connected to?

SL: Very connected. Those are some of my favorite films: *Bicycle Thieves, Open City, Shoeshine, Paisà.* Those are the great films [by] Roberto Rossellini, Vittorio de Sica.

LC: Why do you think these films worked so well?

SL: Because they took the camera out of the studio and shot and documented what people were going through right after the war. Another great thing: out of all the films I mentioned, one of the main characters is a child, and all of this [film] shows the effect of war on children.

LC: Like [Martin] Scorsese, in a way, particular gems of your body of work have been overlooked by the Oscars. Is it something you think about?

SL: Other people may think about it, but that's not why I make films. The work is what matters, and in my experience, people that go into [film-making] thinking, "I'm doing it. I'm directing this film to get a nomination. I'm taking this role to get a nomination"—that's dealing with the devil. With me, I'm just trying to do the best I can at that particular moment, with the story that we have, and the resources that we have. Any type of awards, recognition, or acknowledgment that comes from that work [is icing on the cake]. It's always good to be recognized, but that is not first and foremost. That is not paramount. You never put awards in front of the work.

LC: From the beginning of your career, you were known to consistently work with a multiracial production team. Do you feel like that extra fight was worth it ultimately?

SL: It was definitely worth it. I'm not trying to say I was doing anything abnormal. I was doing what I needed to do. That was a constant battle going back and forth. We had to go to the mat a couple of times, but it was worth it because now there are many, many people working today, behind the camera, in an industry and for unions that, historically, [have] not been as open. I felt that the little power I had should be used to try and get as many of us in there. It's not just African Americans. It's [been about helping to bring onboard] Hispanics, women . . . you know, Latinos, Asian Americans. I really wanted to add diversity to the ranks of the film-makers here in New York City. It was not common to see on these sets any black [crew member]. That's changed now, and that didn't happen overnight. We really, really had to put our foot down in many instances.

LC: What's out there on your horizon, regarding film projects or otherwise?

SL: Right now we're editing a documentary we did on Kobe Bryant for ESPN that takes place in one game on April 13 this past season. And we had thirty cameras on him the entire game. I also just filmed the final performance of the Broadway musical *Passing Strange,* and we're editing that too. So those two things are in the can, shot already, and now we're finishing. My next film is . . . [*smiles*] I don't know.

LC: Given its specialness, do you think it's going to be an energized campaign for *Passing Strange?*

SL: Most of the time, when a show closes, it's gone. There's no record of it. But there will be one of this.

LC: With all the expressiveness in the film, can you talk about working at times with the Italian language, translating and distilling it?

SL: You know, I have to keep going back to the source. Therefore, I have to keep thanking my main man James McBride, who wrote a great book and a true story; and we landed on this. [One random day] I was looking for something to read. There are many books on the shelf [before me]. The spirits told me to take this book off the shelf. There could've been another book. Hellooo! [It was this one!] That's why the fact that this film got made is a miracle. The fact of [Senator] Barack Obama [being the Democratic presidential nominee] is a miracle. I think that anyone who believes in God, who believes in religion, that alone allows [the existence of] miracles.

LC: Speaking of miracles and legacies, you've spoken about [the pioneer African American filmmaker] Oscar Micheaux being a key inspiration, a "Godfather of Independent Film." Can you share a few words on him?

SL: Well, Oscar Micheaux is the person I first learned about when dealing with film. He's a man I still can't even *fathom* the difficulties he had, in doing films for his community. [It's a testament to the fact that] that Negroes back then liked films too, and wanted to see representative roles of who we are. He spent the rest of his life, no matter how hard of a struggle it was, getting those films done and providing entertainment for people—all people. So, he's the godfather, and at the end of the day, you [look back and] have Oscar, Melvin Van Peebles, Gordon Parks, Ossie Davis, Michael Schultz! . . . These are the guys who paved the way . . . *for me*!

Joe's Bed-Stuy Barbershop: We Cut Heads (1983)
Production: 40 Acres and a Mule Filmworks, Tisch School of the Arts, New
    York University
Director: Spike Lee
Producers: Spike Lee and Zimmie Shelton
Screenplay: Spike Lee
Cinematography: Ernest Dickerson
Editor: Spike Lee
Music: Bill Lee
Cast: Monty Ross, Donna Bailey, Stuart Smith
Color
60 min.

She's Gotta Have It (1986)
Production: 40 Acres and a Mule Filmworks
Director: Spike Lee
Producer: Spike Lee
Screenplay: Spike Lee
Cinematography: Ernest Dickerson
Editor: Spike Lee
Sound: Barry Brown
Music: Bill Lee
Cast: Tracy Camilla Johns, Tommy Redmond Hicks, John Canada Terrell,
    Spike Lee
Black and white, color
84 min.

School Daze (1988)
Production: 40 Acres and a Mule Filmworks, Columbia Pictures
Director: Spike Lee
Executive Producer: Grace Blake

Producer: Spike Lee
Coproducers: Loretha C. Jones and Monty Ross
Screenplay: Spike Lee
Cinematography: Ernest Dickerson
Editor: Barry Brown
Music: Bill Lee
Cast: Laurence Fishburne, Giancarlo Esposito, Tisha Campbell-Martin,
    Kyme
Color
121 min.

Do the Right Thing (1989)
Production: 40 Acres and a Mule Filmworks
Director: Spike Lee
Producer: Spike Lee
Coproducer: Monty Ross
Line Producer: Jon Kilik
Screenplay: Spike Lee
Cinematography: Ernest Dickerson
Editor: Barry Brown
Music: Bill Lee
Cast: Danny Aiello, Spike Lee, Giancarlo Esposito, Bill Nunn, Joie Lee,
    John Turturro, Richard Edson, Rosie Perez
Color
120 min.

Mo' Better Blues (1990)
Production: 40 Acres and a Mule Filmworks
Director: Spike Lee
Producer: Spike Lee
Coproducer: Monty Ross
Line Producer: Jon Kilik
Screenplay: Spike Lee
Cinematography: Ernest Dickerson
Editor: Sam Pollard
Music: Bill Lee
Cast: Denzel Washington, Spike Lee, Wesley Snipes, Joie Lee, Cynda
    Williams
Color
129 min.

Jungle Fever (1991)
Production: 40 Acres and a Mule Filmworks, Universal Pictures
Director: Spike Lee
Producer: Spike Lee
Coproducer: Monty Ross
Line Producer: Jon Kilik
Screenplay: Spike Lee
Cinematography: Ernest Dickerson
Editor: Sam Pollard
Music: Terence Blanchard
Cast: Wesley Snipes, Annabella Sciora, Lonette McKee, Samuel L. Jackson,
   John Turturro
Color
132 min.

Malcolm X (1992)
Production: 40 Acres and a Mule Filmworks, Largo International, JVC
   Entertainment Networks
Director: Spike Lee
Producers: Spike Lee, Marvin Worth, and Ahmed Murad
Coproducers: Monty Ross, Preston Holmes, and Jon Kilik
Associate Producer: Fernando Sulichin
Screenplay: Spike Lee and Arnold Perl
Cinematography: Ernest Dickerson
Editor: Barry Brown
Music: Terence Blanchard
Cast: Denzel Washington, Spike Lee, Angela Bassett, Delroy Lindo,
   Albert Hall
Color
202 min.

Crooklyn (1994)
Production: 40 Acres and a Mule Filmworks, Child Hood Productions,
   Universal Pictures
Director: Spike Lee
Executive Producer: Jon Kilik
Producer: Spike Lee
Coproducer: Monty Ross
Associate Producers: Cinqué Lee and Joie Lee
Screenplay: Joie Lee, Cinqué Lee, and Spike Lee
Cinematography: Arthur Jafa
Editor: Barry Brown

Music: Terence Blanchard
Cast: Alfre Woodard, Delroy Lindo, Zelda Harris, Isaiah Washington
Color
115 min.

Clockers (1995)
Production: 40 Acres and a Mule Filmworks, Universal Pictures
Director: Spike Lee
Executive Producers: Monty Ross and Rosalie Swedlin
Producers: Spike Lee, Jon Kilik, and Martin Scorsese
Coproducer: Richard Price
Screenplay: Richard Price and Spike Lee
Cinematography: Malik Hassan Sayeed
Editor: Sam Pollard
Music: Terence Blanchard
Cast: Mekhi Phifer, Delroy Lindo, Harvey Keitel, John Turturro,
   Isaiah Washington
Color
128 min.

Girl 6 (1996)
Production: 40 Acres and a Mule Filmworks, Fox Searchlight Pictures
Director: Spike Lee
Executive Producer: Jon Kilik
Producer: Spike Lee
Associate Producer: Cirri Nottage
Screenplay: Suzan-Lori Parks
Cinematography: Malik Hassan Sayeed
Editor: Sam Pollard
Cast: Theresa Randle, Spike Lee, Isaiah Washington
Color
108 min.

Get on the Bus (1996)
Production: 40 Acres and a Mule Filmworks, 15 Black Men
Director: Spike Lee
Executive Producer: Spike Lee
Producers: Bill Borden, Reuben Cannon, and Barry Rosenbush
Screenplay: Reggie Rock Blythewood
Cinematography: Elliot Davis
Editor: Leander T. Sales
Music: Terence Blanchard

Cast: Ossie Davis, Charles S. Dutton, Andre Braugher, Thomas Jefferson Byrd, Roger Guevner Smith, Hill Harper
Color
120 min.

4 Little Girls (1997)
Production: 40 Acres and a Mule Filmworks, HBO
Director: Spike Lee
Executive Producer: Sheila Nevins
Producers: Spike Lee and Sam Pollard
Associate Producer: Michele Foreman
Coordinating Producer: Jacqueline Glover
Cinematography: Ellen Kuras
Editor: Sam Pollard
Music: Terence Blanchard
Cast: Maxine McNair, Chris McNair
Color
102 min.

He Got Game (1998)
Production: 40 Acres and a Mule Filmworks, Touchstone Pictures
Director: Spike Lee
Producers: Spike Lee and Jon Kilik
Supervising Producer: Sonya Burres
Screenplay: Spike Lee
Cinematography: Ellen Kuras and Malik Hassan Sayeed
Editor: Barry Brown
Music: Aaron Copland
Cast: Denzel Washington, Ray Allen, Rosario Dawson
Color
136 min.

Freak (1998)
Television Film
Production: Lower East Side Films
Director: Spike Lee
Executive Producers: John Leguizamo and Robert Morton
Co-executive Producer: David Bar Katz
Producer: Denis Biggs
Associate Producers: Robert Enriguez and Heather Maidat
Coordinating Producer: Krysia Pionka
Screenplay: John Leguizamo and David Bar Katz
Cinematography: Malik Hassan Sayeed

Editor: Barry Brown
Cast: John Leguizamo
Color
108 min.

Summer of Sam (1999)
Production: 40 Acres and a Mule Filmworks, Touchstone Pictures,
    Hostage Productions
Director: Spike Lee
Executive Producers: Jeri Carroll-Colicchio and Michael Imperioli
Producers: Spike Lee and Jon Kilik
Screenplay: Victor Colicchio, Michael Imperioli, and Spike Lee
Cinematography: Ellen Kuras
Editor: Barry Brown
Music: Terence Blanchard
Cast: John Leguizamo, Mira Sorvino, Adrien Brody, Jennifer Esposito
Color
142 min.

The Original Kings of Comedy (2000)
Production: 40 Acres and a Mule Filmworks, Latham Entertainment, MTV
    Films
Director: Spike Lee
Executive Producer: Van Toffler
Producers: David Gale, Walter Latham, and Spike Lee
Coproducer: Butch Robinson
Associate Producers: Rylyn DeMaris and Angelia Price
Screenplay: Steve Harvey, D. L. Hughley, Cedric the Entertainer,
    and Bernie Mac
Cinematography: Malik Hassan Sayeed
Editor: Barry Brown
Cast: Steve Harvey, D. L. Hughley, Cedric the Entertainer, Bernie Mac
Color
115 min.

Bamboozled (2000)
Production: 40 Acres and a Mule Filmworks, New Line Cinema
Director: Spike Lee
Producers: Spike Lee and Jon Kilik
Associate Producer: Kisha Imani Cameron
Screenplay: Spike Lee
Cinematography: Ellen Kuras
Editor: Sam Pollard

Music: Terence Blanchard
Cast: Damon Wayans, Savion Glover, Jada Pinkett Smith, Tommy Davidson,
    Michael Rapaport, Mos Def
Color
135 min.

A Huey P. Newton Story (2001)
Television Documentary
Production: 40 Acres and a Mule Filmworks, Luna Ray Films,
    Lyrical Knockout Entertainment
Director: Spike Lee
Producers: Steven Adams and Marc Henry Johnson
Associate Producers: Christopher Black, Raoul Juneja,
    and Virginia McCollum
Screenplay: Roger Guenver Smith
Cinematography: Ellen Kuras
Editor: Barry Brown
Cast: Roger Guenver Smith, Georgina Keajra
Color
86 min.

Jim Brown: All American (2002)
Television Documentary
Production: 40 Acres and a Mule Filmworks, HBO Sports
Director: Spike Lee
Executive Producers: Rick Bernstein and Ross Greenburg
Producer: Spike Lee
Coproducers: Mike Ellis and Sam Pollard
Cinematography: Ellen Kuras
Editor: Mark Fason
Music: Terence Blanchard
Cast: Jim Brown, Ralph Wiley, Art Modell
Color
140 min.

25th Hour (2002)
Production: 40 Acres and a Mule Filmworks, 25th Hour Productions,
    Gamut Films
Director: Spike Lee
Executive Producer: Nick Wechsler
Producers: Spike Lee, Jon Kilik, Julia Chasman, and Tobey Maguire
Coproducer: Edward Norton
Associate Producer: Jeff Sommerville

Screenplay: David Benioff
Cinematography: Rodrigo Prieto
Editor: Barry Brown
Music: Terence Blanchard
Cast: Edward Norton, Rosario Dawson, Brian Cox, Philip Seymour Hoffman,
   Barry Pepper, Anna Paquin
Color
135 min.

She Hate Me (2004)
Production: 40 Acres and a Mule Filmworks, Rule 8
Director: Spike Lee
Executive Producers: Jean Cazes and Djamel Debbouze
Producers: Spike Lee, Preston Holmes, and Fernando Sulichin
Coproducer: Craig Spitzer
Screenplay: Michael Genet and Spike Lee
Cinematography: Matthew Libatique
Editor: Barry Brown
Music: Terence Blanchard
Cast: Anthony Mackie, Kerry Washington, Ellen Barkin, Dania Ramirez,
   Jim Brown, Lonette McKee, John Turturro, Monica Bellucci
Color
138 min.

Sucker Free City (2004)
Television Pilot
Production: 40 Acres and a Mule Filmworks
Director: Spike Lee
Executive Producers: Sam Kitt and Spike Lee
Co-executive Producer: Alex Tse
Producer: Preston Holmes
Screenplay: Alex Tse
Cinematography: César Charlone
Editor: Barry Brown
Music: Terence Blanchard
Cast: Ben Crowley, Ken Leung, Anthony Mackie
Color
113 min.

Inside Man (2006)
Production: 40 Acres and a Mule Filmworks, Universal Pictures,
   Imagine Entertainment
Director: Spike Lee

Executive Producers: Jon Kilik, Daniel Rosenberg, Karen Kehela Sherwood, and Kim Roth
Producer: Brian Grazer
Coproducer: Jonathan Filley
Screenplay: Russell Gewirtz
Cinematography: Matthew Libatique
Editor: Barry Brown
Music: Terence Blanchard
Cast: Denzel Washington, Clive Owen, Jodie Foster, Chiwetel Ejiofor
Color
129 min.

When the Levees Broke: A Requiem in Four Acts (2006)
Television Documentary Miniseries
Production: 40 Acres and a Mule Filmworks, HBO
Director: Spike Lee
Executive Producer: Sheila Nevins
Producers: Spike Lee and Sam Pollard
Supervising Producer: Jacqueline Glover
Cinematography: Cliff Charles
Editors: Barry Brown, Geeta Gandbhir, Nancy Novak, and Sam Pollard
Music: Terence Blanchard
Cast: Shelton Alexander, Harry Belafonte, Michael Eric Dyson, Wendell Pierce
Color
255 min.

Miracle at St. Anna (2008)
Production: 40 Acres and a Mule Filmworks, On My Own, Rai Cinema
Director: Spike Lee
Executive Producers: Jon Kilik and Marco Valerio Pugini
Producers: Roberto Cicutto, Spike Lee, and Luigi Musini
Line Producers: Dave Pomier and Butch Robinson
Screenplay: James McBride
Cinematography: Matthew Libatique
Editor: Barry Brown
Music: Terence Blanchard
Cast: Laz Alonso, Derek Luke, Michael Ealy, Joseph Gordon-Levitt, Valentina Cervi
Color
160 min.

Kobe Doin' Work (2009)
Television Documentary
Production: 40 Acres and a Mule Filmworks, ESPN Films
Director: Spike Lee
Executive Producers: Keith Clinkscales, John Dahl, Joan Lynch,
  and Connor Schell
Producer: Spike Lee
Line Producer: Butch Robinson
Cinematography: Matthew Libatique
Editor: Barry Brown
Cast: Kobe Bryant, Lamar Odom, Phil Jackson
Color
84 min.

If God Is Willing and da Creek Don't Rise (2010)
Television Documentary Miniseries
Production: 40 Acres and a Mule Filmworks, HBO
Director: Spike Lee
Executive Producer: Sheila Nevins
Producers: Spike Lee and Sam Pollard
Supervising Producer: Jacqueline Glover
Line Producer: Butch Robinson
Cinematography: Cliff Charles
Editors: Geeta Gandbhir and Sam Pollard
Music: Terence Blanchard
Cast: Calvin Mackie, Tanya Harris, Ray Nagin, Brad Pitt
Color
240 min.

Red Hook Summer (2012)
Production: 40 Acres and a Mule Filmworks
Director: Spike Lee
Producer: Spike Lee
Screenplay: Spike Lee and James McBride
Line Producer: Tim Stacker
Cinematography: Kerwin DeVonish
Editor: Hye Mee Na
Music: Bruce Hornsby
Cast: Limary Agosto, Turron Kofi Alleyne, Daniel Breaker
Color
121 min.

Bibliography

Abrams, Jerold J. "Transcendence and Sublimity in Spike Lee's Signature Shot." In *The Philosophy of Spike Lee.* Ed. Mark T. Conard. Lexington: University Press of Kentucky, 2011. 187–99.

Adorno. Theodor W. *Minima Moralia: Reflections from Damaged Life.* Trans. E. F. N. Jephcott. New York: Verso, 1978.

Badiou, Alain. *Number and Numbers.* Trans. Robin Mackay. Malden, Mass.: Polity, 2008.

———. *Theory of the Subject.* Trans. Bruno Bosteels. New York: Continuum, 2009.

Barthes, Roland. "The Third Meaning." In *Image Music Text.* Trans. Stephen Heath. New York: Hill and Wang, 1977. 52–68.

Bellour, Raymond. "To Enunciate (on *Marnie*)." Trans. Bertrand Augst and Hilary Radner. Rev. by Constance Penley. In *The Analysis of Film.* Ed. Constance Penley. Bloomington: Indiana University Press, 2000. 217–37.

Butler, Judith. *The Psychic Life of Power.* Stanford, Calif.: Stanford University Press, 1997.

Cardullo, Bert. "Law of the Jungle." *Hudson Review* 44.4 (1992): 639–47.

Chidester, Phil, and Jamel Santa Cruze Bell. "'Say the Right Thing': Spike Lee, *Bamboozled,* and the Future of Satire in a Postmodern World." In *Fight the Power!: The Spike Lee Reader.* Ed. Janice D. Hamlet and Robin R. Means Coleman. New York: Peter Lang, 2009. 203–22.

Childs, Erica Chito. *Fade to Black and White: Interracial Images in Popular Culture.* Lanham, Md.: Rowman and Littlefield, 2009.

Coleman, Robin R. Means, and Janice D. Hamlet. Introduction to *Fight the Power!: The Spike Lee Reader.* Ed. Janice D. Hamlet and Robin R. Means Coleman. New York: Peter Lang, 2009. xix–xxxi.

Conard, Mark T., ed. *The Philosophy of Spike Lee.* Lexington: University Press of Kentucky, 2011.

Copjec, Joan. *Imagine There's No Woman: Ethics and Sublimation.* Cambridge: Massachusetts Institute of Technology Press, 2002.

Daileader, Celia R. *Racism, Misogyny, and the Othello Myth: Interracial Couples from Shakespeare to Spike Lee*. Cambridge: Cambridge University Press, 2005.

Delue, Rachel Ziady. "Envisioning Race in Spike Lee's *Bamboozled*." In *Fight the Power!: The Spike Lee Reader*. Ed. Janice D. Hamlet and Robin R. Means Coleman. New York: Peter Lang, 2009. 61–88.

Denzin, Norman K. "Spike's Place." In *Fight the Power!: The Spike Lee Reader*. Ed. Janice D. Hamlet and Robin R. Means Coleman. New York: Peter Lang, 2009. 103–25.

Finnegan, Elizabeth Hope. "(Still) Fighting the Power: Public Space and the Unspeakable Privacy of the Other in *Do the Right Thing*." In *The Philosophy of Spike Lee*. Ed. Mark T. Conard. Lexington: University Press of Kentucky, 2011. 75–94.

Flory, Dan. "*Bamboozled*: Philosophy through Blackface." In *The Philosophy of Spike Lee*. Ed. Mark T. Conard. Lexington: University Press of Kentucky, 2011. 164–83.

———. *Philosophy, Black Film, Film Noir*. University Park: Penn State University Press, 2008.

Fuchs, Cynthia, ed. *Spike Lee Interviews*. Jackson: University Press of Mississippi, 2002.

Gabbard, Krin. "Race and Reappropriation: Spike Lee Meets Aaron Copland." *American Music* 18.4 (2000): 370–90.

Gabbard, Krin. "Signifyin(g) the Phallus: *Mo' Better Blues* and Representations of the Jazz Trumpet." *Cinema Journal* 32.1 (1992): 43–62.

Gaines, Mikal J. "Spike's Blues: Re-imagining Blues Ideology for the Cinema." In *Fight the Power!: The Spike Lee Reader*. Ed. Janice D. Hamlet and Robin R. Means Coleman. New York: Peter Lang, 2009. 147–70.

Guerrero, Ed. *Do the Right Thing*. London: British Film Institute, 2001.

Hamlet, Janice D., and Robin R. Means Coleman, eds. *Fight the Power!: The Spike Lee Reader*. New York: Peter Lang, 2009.

Harris, Erich Leon. "The Demystification of Spike Lee." In *Spike Lee Interviews*. Ed. Cynthia Fuchs. Jackson: University Press of Mississippi, 2002. 126–38.

Harris, William A. "Cultural Engineering and the Films of Spike Lee." In *Fight the Power!: The Spike Lee Reader*. Ed. Janice D. Hamlet and Robin R. Means Coleman. New York: Peter Lang, 2009. 23–40.

Harrison-Kahan, Lori. "Inside *Inside Man*: Spike Lee and Post-9/11 Entertainment." *Cinema Journal* 50.1 (2010): 39–58.

Heath, Stephen. *Questions of Cinema*. Bloomington: Indiana University Press, 1981.

Hoffman, Karen D. "Feminists and 'Freaks': *She's Gotta Have It* and *Girl 6*." In *The Philosophy of Spike Lee*. Ed. Mark T. Conard. Lexington: University Press of Kentucky, 2011. 106–22.

hooks, bell. *Reel to Real: Race, Sex, and Class at the Movies*. New York: Routledge, 1996.

Johnson, Victoria E. "Polyphony and Cultural Expression: Interpreting Musical Traditions in *Do the Right Thing*." In *Spike Lee's* Do the Right Thing. Ed. Mark A. Reid. New York: Cambridge University Press, 1997. 50–72.

Karatani, Kojin. *Architecture as Metaphor: Language, Number, Money*. Trans. Sabu Kosho. Cambridge: Massachusetts Institute of Technology Press, 1995.

Karenga, Maulana. "The Million Man March/Day of Absence Mission Statement." In *Million Man March/Day of Absence: A Commemorative Anthology*. Ed. Haki R. Madhubuti and Maulana Karenga. Chicago: Third World Press, 1996. 5–7.

Kellner, Douglas. "Aesthetics, Ethics, and Politics in the Films of Spike Lee." In *Spike Lee's* Do the Right Thing. Ed. Mark A. Reid. New York: Cambridge University Press, 1997. 73–106.

Khoury, George. "Big Words: An Interview with Spike Lee." In *Spike Lee Interviews*. Ed. Cynthia Fuchs. Jackson: University Press of Mississippi, 2002. 146–54.

Lacan, Jacques. *The Seminar of Jacques Lacan, Book VII: The Ethics of Psychoanalysis, 1959–1960*. Ed. Jacques-Alain Miller. Trans. Dennis Porter. New York: Norton, 1992.

———. "The Subversion of the Subject and the Dialectic of Desire in the Freudian Unconscious." In *Écrits: The First Complete Edition in English*. Trans. Bruce Fink. New York: Norton, 2006. 671–702.

Lee, Spike, and Kaleem Aftab. *That's My Story and I'm Sticking to It*. New York: Norton, 2005.

Locke, John. *Two Treatises of Government*. New York: Cambridge University Press, 1988.

Lukács, Georg. *History and Class Consciousness: Studies in Marxist Dialectics*. Trans. Rodney Livingstone. Cambridge: Massachusetts Institute of Technology Press, 1971.

MacFarland, Douglas. "The Symbolism of Blood in *Clockers*." In *The Philosophy of Spike Lee*. Ed. Mark T. Conard. Lexington: University Press of Kentucky, 2011. 3–14.

Massood, Paula J., ed. *The Spike Lee Reader*. Philadelphia: Temple University Press, 2007.

Metz, Christian. *The Imaginary Signifier: Psychoanalysis and Cinema*. Trans. Celia Britton, Annwyl Williams, Ben Brewster, and Alfred Guzzetti. Bloomington: Indiana University Press, 1982.

Nasio, Juan-David. *Le Fantasme: Le plasir de lire Lacan*. Paris: Petite Bibliothèque Payot, 2005.

Neroni, Hilary. "The Nonsensical Smile of the Torturer: Documentary Form and the Logic of Enjoyment." *Studies in Documentary Film* 3.3 (2009): 245–57.

Palmer, R. Barton. "Monsters and Moralism in *Summer of Sam*." In *The Phi-*

losophy of Spike Lee. Ed. Mark T. Conard. Lexington: University Press of Kentucky, 2011. 54–71.

Patton, Tracey Owens, and Deborah McGriff. "'Ya Been Took, Ya Been Hoodwinked, Ya Been Bamboozled': Mau-Maus, Diaspora, and the Mediated Misrepresentation of Blacks." In *Fight the Power!: The Spike Lee Reader.* Ed. Janice D. Hamlet and Robin R. Means Coleman. New York: Peter Lang, 2009. 89–102.

Paulin, Diana R. "De-Essentializing Interracial Representations: Black and White Border-Crossings in Spike Lee's *Jungle Fever* and Octavia Butler's *Kindred.*" *Cultural Critique* 36 (1997): 165–93.

Reid, Mark A., ed. *Spike Lee's Do the Right Thing.* New York: Cambridge University Press, 1997.

Saltman, Benjamin. Rev. of *Jungle Fever. Film Quarterly* 45.2 (1991–92): 37–41.

Samuels, Allison. "Spike's Minstral Show." In *Spike Lee Interviews.* Ed. Cynthia Fuchs. Jackson: University Press of Mississippi, 2002. 187–88.

Santner, Eric L. *The Royal Remains: The People's Two Bodies and the Endgames of Sovereignty.* Chicago: University of Chicago Press, 2011.

Smith-Shomade, Beretta E. "'I Be Smackin' my Hoes': Paradox and Authenticity in *Bamboozled.*" In *The Spike Lee Reader.* Ed. Paula J. Massood. Philadelphia: Temple University Press, 2007. 228–42.

Sragow, Michael. "Black Like Spike." In *Spike Lee Interviews.* Ed. Cynthia Fuchs. Jackson: University Press of Mississippi, 2002. 188–98.

Stempel, Tom. *American Audiences on Movies and Moviegoing.* Lexington: University Press of Kentucky, 2001.

Stevens, Maurice E. "Subject to Countermemory: Disavowal and Black Manhood in Spike Lee's *Malcolm X.*" In *Fight the Power!: The Spike Lee Reader.* Ed. Janice D. Hamlet and Robin R. Means Coleman. New York: Peter Lang, 2009. 321–41.

Sundstrom, Ronald R. "Fevered Desires and Interracial Intimacies in *Jungle Fever.*" In *The Philosophy of Spike Lee.* Ed. Mark T. Conard. Lexington: University Press of Kentucky, 2011. 144–63.

Thompson, Kristin. *Eisenstein's "Ivan the Terrible": A Neoformalist Analysis.* Princeton, N.J.: Princeton University Press, 1981.

Watkins, S. Craig. "Reel Men: *Get on the Bus* and the Shifting Terrain of Black Masculinities." In *The Spike Lee Reader.* Ed. Paula J. Massood. Philadelphia: Temple University Press, 2007. 142–58.

Willis, Sharon. *High Contrast: Race and Gender in Contemporary Hollywood Film.* Durham, N.C.: Duke University Press, 1997.

Wollen, Peter. "Godard and Counter Cinema: *Vent d'est.*" *Afterimage* 4 (1972): 6–17.

Žižek, Slavoj. *Tarrying with the Negative: Kant, Hegel, and the Critique of Ideology.* Durham, N.C.: Duke University Press, 1993.

Zupančič, Alenka. *Ethics of the Real: Kant, Lacan.* New York: Verso, 2000.

Index

Todd McGowan is associate professor of English
at the University of Vermont and author of
Out of Time: The Ethics of Atemporal Cinema.

Books in the series
Contemporary Film Directors

The University of Illinois Press
is a founding member of the
Association of American University Presses.

———————————————————

Designed by Paula Newcomb
Composed in 10/13 New Caledonia LT Std
with Helvetica Neue display
by Celia Shapland
at the University of Illinois Press
Manufactured by Sheridan Books, Inc.

University of Illinois Press
1325 South Oak Street
Champaign, IL 61820-6903
www.press.uillinois.edu